the world:

A Gateway

the world:
A
Gateway

Commentaries on the Mumonkan

by Albert Low

Charles E. Tuttle Co., Inc.
Boston • Rutland, Vermont • Tokyo

Published by Charles E. Tuttle Co., Inc. of Rutland, Vermont
and Tokyo, Japan with editorial offices at 153 Milk St., 5th floor
Boston, MA 02109

Library of Congress Cataloging–in–Publication Data

Low, Albert.
   The world : a gateway : commentaries on the Mumonkan / by
Albert Low
      p. cm.
   Includes excerpts from Diamond sutra and Prajnaparamita.
   ISBN 0-8048-3046-0
   I. Hui-k'ai, 1183-1260. Wu-men kuan.   II. Title.
BQ9289.H843L69   1995
294.3'4—dc20
                                                      94-46614
                                                         CIP

First Edition
1 3 5 7 9 10 8 6 4 2

Printed in the United States of America

*dedicated with deep respect
to my students
at the Montreal Zen Center*

Contents

Preface

The *Mumonkan,* first published in China in the thirteenth century A.D., is probably the most accessible of all the collections of koans, and the comments and verses of the compiler, Zen master Mumon, are pithy and to the point. For this reason it is well known and well appreciated among Zen practitioners to this day.

Zen master Mumon was born in 1183 and had Zen master Getsurin as his teacher. It was from Getsurin that Mumon received the koan Mu! He struggled to see into the koan for six long years but was unsuccessful until he finally resolved, come what may, to let nothing stop him from penetrating it. He vowed not to lay down to sleep until he had done so and even went so far as to bang his head against a pillar in order to stay awake and continue his inquiry. Eventually he did break through and wrote the following verse in celebration:

> *Out of a broad blue sky, the sun shining bright, came*
> *   a clap of thunder!*
> *All beings through great nature opened wide their eyes*
> *All the many living things bow down in wonder*
> *Mount Sumeru, awry, dances a jig.*

He compiled the *Mumonkan* when he was head monk at Ryushoji monastery. He later became abbot of Hoinyuji Zen Temple and died at the age of seventy-eight in the year 1260. His death poem was:

> *Emptiness is unborn*
> *Emptiness does not die*

Preface

If you know emptiness
You and emptiness do not differ.

The version of the *Mumonkan* presented here comes from one compiled by Philip Kapleau, Roshi, the teacher with whom I practiced for twenty years. In making up his version he consulted translations of the *Mumonkan* made by R.H. Blyth and Zenkei Shibayama. I have also consulted other translations and have used my own years of work on the koans, both as a teacher and as a student, in an effort to present the koans, comments, and verses as clearly as possible using the idiom of today. The versions of the koans that are given here are therefore, in the main, original and my own.

In the appendices I have provided selections from the *Diamond Sutra,* all of the *Prajnaparamita Hridaya,* and also a short excerpt from Hwa Yen taken from *The Buddhist Teaching of Totality.* The excerpts from the *Diamond Sutra* are also a compilation from several sources. I have included these texts to provide some background to the koans. Zen monks and masters would have been familiar with them and with a number of other sutras; the *Diamond Sutra* and the *Prajnaparamita Hridaya* have the merit of being brief and to the point.

This work is not intended to be a scholarly treatise but rather a working manual. Now and again I have made notes and, where necessary, have cited the sources from which quotes were taken. This kind of thing has been kept to a minimum. I have often cited two other works in the commentaries, the *Hekiganroku* and *I Am That,* a collection of conversations that the Hindu master, Nisargadatta Maharaj, had with various people over the years. It has been helpful to use koans from the *Hekiganroku,* either as a complement to or in contrast to koans under review. The publication of the *Hekiganroku,* or *Blue Cliff Record,* as it is also known, preceded that of the *Mumonkan* by about a hundred years. The koans were compiled by Zen master Setcho who also wrote a verse for each one. Most of the cases had an introductory word from another Zen master, Engo, who also made trenchant comments on the koans and their protagonists.

Nisargadatta Maharaj died in 1982 after having lived in Bombay for about eighty years. He was a remarkable man who came to very deep awakening only two or three years after having met his teacher. One of the remarkable things about him is his saying, "My teacher said to me that I was whole and complete, and I believed him." This deep faith made it possible for Nisargadatta to attain an awakening that few can hope to attain. The comments that he made in the conversations he had with his visitors are so to the point, so direct and clear, that it is difficult not to use them on occasion.

The comments have been written with an eye to practice, to helping people find a toe-hold on the sheer face of the koans and so be able to begin the work of finding their way to the summit to which all koans lead. With this in mind, I have not followed the usual practice of making separate comments on the case, the commentary, and the verse. These kinds of remarks have always seemed to me to be unnecessarily pedantic and often end in the author/translator commenting for the sake of commenting rather than saying what is most helpful to the reader.

The comments have been made with the interested reader (one who does not necessarily intend to practice) in mind as well as the person who is working, or who has already worked, through the koans with a teacher. One thing I try to emphasize at the Montreal Zen Center is that koan practice is more like a koan appreciation class rather than like racing through an obstacle course. With this in view, one's appreciation of a koan will deepen each time one returns to it.

To truly grasp a koan, however, kensho, or awakening, is necessary, and one must understand that each koan is of equal importance and, ultimately, of equal difficulty. Furthermore, each must be seen into. Each koan, in other words, calls for its own kensho. Yasutani Roshi used to insist that each koan is an initiating koan and the fact that the koan Mu! appears first in the collection was probably due more to Mumon's liking for it than for any other reason.

I have used Japanese names throughout this book both for the names of the teachers and also for the names of monasteries and temples. I have two reasons for doing this. Although Zen originated in China, most of us came to the practice through books that were written either by Japanese or by Westerners who had studied and practiced in Japan, so the Japanese names are already familiar. Second, the Japanese language is easier for the Westerner to pronounce and so makes easier reading, although we must never forget the debt of gratitude we owe to the Chinese genius.

Albert Low

Acknowledgments

I should like to pay tribute to the excellent job of editing that my wife, Jean, has done on the manuscript. She has simplified the text considerably and so made it that much more accessible.

I should also like to express gratitude to the Rochester Zen Center for permission to include their version of the *Prajnaparamita,* as Appendix Two, and for permission to use *Lighting a Lamp of the Law,* which is reproduced as Appendix Three.

I should also like to thank Elizabeth Namiesniowski for her fine illustrations.

Sarah Jeffries as editor has done a fine job of pointing up the text and has my sincere thanks.

Finally, I should like to express respect and gratitude to my teacher Philip Kapleau, Roshi, who guided me through the reefs and shoals of Zen practice for so many years.

Dharma gates without number I vow to penetrate.

Introduction

Hearing, seeing, touching and knowing are not one
*   and one;*
Mountains and rivers are not seen in a mirror
The frosty sky, the setting moon—at midnight;
With whom will the serene waters of the lake reflect
the shadows.

—from verse to koan 40 of the *Hekiganroku*

Silence is always present. Even downtown amid the traffic, or during a raging hurricane or bombardment, silence is always present. Silence is presence. By this I mean that silence is not simply the absence of sound or noise, it is not a lack, a deficiency. In the *Surangama Sutra* it asks, "If the bell stops ringing, does the ear stop hearing?" If you meditate on this question you will come to see that true nature, also, is never absent. When the bell stops ringing we hear, not nothing, but presence: presence we can call true nature. But to say we "hear" presence is misleading, because hearing is presence in action; so are seeing, tasting, smelling, and touching. Knowing something, thinking, having ideas and imagining, all are presence in action. But this does not mean that presence hears something else. Presence and hearing are one; presence and something heard are also one. Presence, as can be seen from the very origin of the word, means before something is, *pre* "before," *esse,* "to be"; in other words, before being. Presence is therefore omnipresence and always one.

When we use words, as we are using them now, truth slips through the cracks. Words freeze experience into solid blocks. We try to fit the blocks together with reason and seal them together with logic, but they fit badly, and we cannot help leaving gaps through which the vitality of a situation leaks away. Silence, presence, hearing, something, these are all words and, as such, are part of what we call the world. Yet, as a moment's meditation will show, silence itself is not "out there," nor is presence. It is not "in here" either. To believe the inside of the skull, or the inside of the chest cavity, is in some way nearer truth than "out there," is still to be lost in the building blocks of words. "Out there," "in here": more words and more confusion, where the truth is so simple and direct.

It is just because words can no more hold the truth than a net can hold water that koans are used. Koans are sayings, or doings, of Zen masters, the patriarchs, and Buddha. Take for example the koan: The Sound of One Hand Clapping. In its entirety it reads: "You know the sound of two hands clapping. What is the sound of one hand clapping?" The obvious, intellectual answer is no sound at all! But then what is this no sound? In other words, what is silence? If one is to work on this koan, indeed on any koan, one must *demonstrate* its meaning. Explanatory words, such as "the two hands represent duality, the one hand is unity" or "the sound of one hand is the sound of the true self" are useless. A teacher of Zen would reject them out of hand, all the while demanding a real response. Words talk about true nature and, as it were, hold it at arm's length. One must *become* the sound of one hand to be able to give a real response, and in this way see for oneself that the sound of one hand is the full expression of the master's and one's own awakened state.

Koans Do Not Contain Symbols

As we said, a koan is a saying or doing of a master; it issues directly and spontaneously from the awakened mind. A master's response is like sound coming from a gong that is struck: the gong is struck, sound streams out. We said to see into a koan is to be one with the awakened mind of the master; this is to be one with your own awakened mind. But, again, to talk about being one with your own awakened mind smothers the fire of truth. Words, symbols, parables, signs, all *reflect* the sound of one hand, the way the dew on the grass at morning reflects the light of the sun. In their way words are small miracles, but that which performs the miracle of speech is a greater miracle yet. Koans are about that miracle; or rather they are not about it but are its full manifestation.

Metaphors bring us close to true nature because they point to it. Some are of the opinion that all words are in some way metaphors. Even if this is so, most metaphors are dead and have lost their power to point to the truth. Music is also a language of metaphor and so are dance, gesture, and other art forms. Metaphors make the peculiar claim "this is that" but all the time we know "this is not that. " Shakespeare, for example, speaks of "the slings and arrows of outrageous fortune." This is a powerful metaphor, but we all know perfectly well that fortune has neither slings nor arrows. In a similar way we talk of true nature; but we must be careful because, using a formulation of Buddha, "True nature is not true nature, that is why we call it true nature." True nature in this case is a metaphor; "this is that" "this is not that." When we know intimately the truth of Buddha's formulation, we can use words with impunity. It is said that Buddha uses words as words. This is like an entomologist using a magnifying glass to see an insect, but he does not mistake the glass for the insect. Until we know this intimately and can use words as words, we must beware of words and metaphors, as we beware of scorpions and poisonous snakes, and treat them with the utmost care and respect.

Parables are extended metaphors, and we must not make the mistake of trying to interpret koans as we might interpret parables. This is not to say that parables have no place on the spiritual path. On the contrary, they and metaphors can help enormously to awaken the mind to possibilities that otherwise would remain dormant and unrecognized. But parables can only awaken *possibilities,* they can only take us to the door. We must take yet another step to enter our true home. The danger with parables, as well as with metaphors, and why we must treat them with such caution, is that by awakening possibilities they open new horizons, give birth to new hope. In the radiance of this hope, in the scope of these new possibilities, we all too easily succumb to the mistaken belief that we have found true gold when all we have found are its tracings.

A Koan Is Not an Exercise or Technique
We use a technique or a tool to accomplish something and, similarly, we do exercises, go through a set of actions, mental or physical, to attain some end. But if we look upon awaking as an end or a goal to be accomplished, we deny the truth of presence. We do not have to reach silence or attain it. We do not require any special method to come to silence. Silence is silence, we do not even have to hear it with our ears. By the same token we do not have to do something to attain true nature. For one thing, true nature is

not *something*. For another, all doing, all saying, all techniques stream out of true nature. We think in terms of technique because we are so fascinated by language. A technique is "someone" "doing" "something" "to attain" "something." However, a well-known Buddhist sutra, the *Prajnaparamita Hridaya,* says not "even wisdom can be attained, attainment too is emptiness." "Someone" "doing" "something" "to attain" "something" are all building blocks. All are suspended in presence like dust motes in the ray of sunlight in a darkened room. *No attainment* is the radical teaching of Zen, so radical it is often overlooked, even by those who preach it.

Koans Have No Teaching
Another well-known sutra, the *Diamond Sutra,* is several pages long. It begins with a disciple asking Buddha for his teaching, and the remainder is a response to that request. At one point Buddha asks his disciple, Subhuti, "Has the Tathagata a teaching to enunciate?" Subhuti answers "As I understand Buddha's meaning, there is no formulation of truth called consummation of incomparable enlightenment. Moreover the Tathagata has no formulated teaching to enunciate." *No formulated teaching* to enunciate; how are we to understand this apparent contradiction? The sutra has a number of pages of teaching, yet Subhuti says Buddha has no teaching.

Subhuti helps us to understand by saying, "The Tathagata has said that truth is uncontainable and inexpressible. It neither is nor is it not." A koan too is not a formulation of truth, it too has no teaching. Indeed, not only does it have no teaching, it has no content either. The difference between a teaching made up of words, symbols, metaphors, and so on, and a koan is like the difference between a picture and a window. If you were to look at a Gainsborough painting you could learn a lot about rural England in the artist's time. In contrast, think about a window, which is without content and without teaching. However, all a picture can do is reflect and refract the light. A window lets pour through, unobstructed, the living light itself.

A Koan Is Not a Mantra

A mantra is a common device used in spiritual training. One repeats a word or phrase over and over. The etymology of the word mantra is *man,* which in Sanskrit means "mind," and *tra* "to protect." A mantra therefore protects the mind from the effects of the deep schism in the very heart of being by giving a stable center.

A Christian mantra, made famous by an anonymous writer of *The Way of a Pilgrim,* is, "Lord Jesus Christ have mercy on me, a sinner." It was used by the Desert Fathers of the fourth and fifth centuries who retired to the desert for a life of solitude and prayer. Another Christian mantra is "Ave Maria." In the Buddhist tradition, in a sect called the Pure Land, "Namu Amidha Butsu" is used. It means "Praise to the Buddha of boundless light." At the end of the *Prajnaparamita Hridaya,* which is chanted in many Zen temples and monasteries, the mantra "Gate, gate, paragate, parasamgate, bodhi, svaha!" is used. It means "Gone, gone, gone beyond, gone quite beyond, Bodhi, rejoice!" Bodhi is the living light that streams through the window when we have gone beyond all the stains of the mind. Hindus, Sufis, and Taoists all have their own versions of mantras, and all use beads, or rosaries in the Catholic tradition, as an aid in mantric practice.

Imagine for the moment a leaderless group of restless, agitated people quarreling among themselves, creating feelings of insecurity, hostility, and anxiety. Without a leader to check them tension will rise steadily in the group. Now suppose a leader is appointed and given full authority from a source respected by all members of the group. The power of the group will now be harmonized: tension, restlessness, and insecurity will decline; a feeling of well-being will reign. Such is the role of a mantra.

Although it gives a harmonizing center, a mantra also closes the mind. Indeed, if it is used without adequate supervision by a teacher who has used the mantra himself or herself over a long period of time, it can have a deleterious effect on the mind, closing it off from its source, and effectively blocking all spiritual progress. Hakuin, a famous seventeenth-century Zen master, is particularly critical of indiscriminate use of mantras.

A mantra takes the form of an affirmation, but a koan takes the form of questioning and doubt. This in effect opens the mind. You can prove this yourself right now by simply having a question, any question, come into your mind. Using a koan in this way opens the mind and gives you the chance to go beyond the need for center, to go to the light of the mind. When we start working with a koan, such as Joshu's Mu! (koan 1 in the present series), we do often use it as a mantra just to keep the mind steady. But later with the help of a competent teacher, we bring deeper, more creative levels of the mind into play by arousing the mind without resting it upon anything, and it is from these deeper levels the koan gets its power.

Introduction

Prajna: Arouse the Mind
Without Resting It Upon Anything

The *Diamond Sutra* is important in the Zen Buddhist tradition. It was made popular in China by the sixth-century Zen patriarch Hui Neng, who came to deep awakening when he heard an itinerant monk chanting the lines, "Arouse the mind without resting it upon anything," which come from the *Diamond Sutra*.

This sutra belongs to the *Prajnaparamita* school of Buddhism that burst upon the spiritual scene of India at about the time that the birth of Jesus spread throughout the rest of Asia. *Paramita* means "to cross over to the other side of the ocean of birth and death." The phrase "ocean of birth and death" is used to indicate the restless, stormy, and bitter life of the human being. *Prajna* means "aroused mind." The Sound of One Hand Clapping and Joshu's Mu! both call on prajna for their resolution. In other words, to see into a koan is just that: to arouse the mind without resting it on anything.

We must not be led to believe that arousing the mind in this way is something mystical, however; it is not. It is something quite ordinary. Every night while we sleep deeply without dreams, the mind is not resting on anything, although of course it is not aroused. During the day the mind is constantly aroused, but it is also resting, or clinging to all sorts of things. Prajna is therefore waking sleep. Hakuin wrote of his disappointment at not being able to attain "the state wherein waking and sleeping are the same." The great Hindu teacher Ramana Maharshi also said that *samadhi* is waking sleep. Prajna and samadhi, or *dhyana* as it is known in Zen, are different in emphasis only. Whereas prajna emphasizes arousing the mind, dhyana, or samadhi, emphasizes not resting it on anything. We all know the conditions of sleeping and waking, we just do not know the two together, that is all. In this condition of waking sleep a turnabout in the mind is possible, what is known in Sanskrit as *paravritti*, and in Japanese as *kensho* or *satori*.

Ordinary Mind Is the Way

Zen insists that ordinary mind is the way (see koan 19). The *Diamond Sutra* opens with the following account:

> *One day, at breakfast time, the world-honored one put on his robe and, carrying his bowl, made his way into the great city of Shravasti to beg for his food. In the midst of the city he begged from door to door according to the rule. This done, he returned to his retreat and ate his meal. When he had finished he put away his robe and begging bowl, washed his feet, arranged his seat, and sat down (see Appendix 1).*

This is the description of a very ordinary state of mind. The word Buddha originally just meant waking up from sleep, and only gradually did it acquire the more exalted meaning of spiritual awakening. In English we have the expression "to come to." For example, should one faint one would later come to; or one is walking along a street in a dreamy state and suddenly one comes to. This ordinary mind is the foundation of Zen practice.

Working On Koans

Each koan in its own way opens onto the koan of everyday mind. Koans are not tests of our spiritual strength or progress; to use them as criteria for determining if a person is ready to teach others, as is often done, is to abuse them.

Introduction

Deep within our minds is a schism, a basic double bind. The word exist means "to stand outside of oneself," from *ex* "outside of" and *sistere,* "to stand," thus to be separated from oneself. Yet all the while Buddhism affirms that we are whole and complete and cannot possibly be otherwise. How is it possible then to exist, to be outside of oneself? The illogic and impossibility of our situation is mirrored one way or another in all koans.

To work on koans we must have utmost faith that they are indeed resolvable on their own terms, that they are in their own way intensely meaningful. Therefore we should not say such things as koans are so phrased that they deliberately throw sand in our eyes to force us to open our mind's eye and see the world and everything in it without distortion, because this can create problems. Although koans have no content they are not mindless mumbles. Moreover, because they open onto the koan of everyday mind we do not have to evoke any special state of mind such as a trance, or any so-called elevated spiritual state of mind to work with them.

A koan is not a Chinese enigma, but a question of life and death, of our own spiritual life and death. Working on a koan is to work on ourselves and the first thing we must do is to make it our own. The koan must in some way open up our own deep torment or dilemma. Unless it does this it will be seen simply as an exercise to strengthen concentration, to come to awakening, or to achieve some other result. As such an exercise it will not be able to engage our heart and mind in their entirety and so will never yield its secret. Therefore to make it our own we should alter it, add to it, subtract from it, until we have absorbed ourselves in it enough so that it is part of our selves. Although the koan must ultimately be addressed and resolved as given and on its own terms, by working it around it becomes accessible, something that it rarely is when one first reads it.

Faith, Doubt and Perseverance
Hakuin said that to practice Zen one needs great faith, great doubt, and great determination.

Faith
Presence is never absent, so we always work on a koan knowing fully its import. In other words, our aim is not simply to find out something we did not know. To repeat, koans do not contain teaching. Therefore we do not start from the standpoint of "I don't know, I must find out." Rather we start from the point of "I know; how does this koan help me to express that knowing?" This "I know" is the full expression of faith. A basic teaching of all schools of Buddhism is that from the beginning all beings are Buddha,[1] and insofar as Buddha means awakened one, or knowing one, *each of us does know,* but this knowing is hidden in the many sheaths that make up our repertoire of knowledge and experience. Someone asked Yasutani Roshi, "What is the difference between you and me?" Yasutani replied, "There is no difference except I know it." A beginner and a master are not different except the master has liberated knowing from its sheaths, whereas the beginner always knows something. Great faith is therefore not great faith in Buddha, in Zen, in a teacher. Buddha, Zen, and teacher are all potential sheaths that once more can trap knowing and crystallize it into being "something." Great faith is great faith in oneself; not oneself as an isolated, separate individual, but oneself as

---

[1] See Hakuin's "Chant in Praise of Zazen."

Introduction

Buddha. To appreciate this fully one must be able to appreciate the Christian mystic who said, "If faith, then faith."

Doubt

Another basic requirement for working on a koan, in particular a breakthrough koan, is the doubt sensation. We have said that deep in our hearts is a schism, a contradiction. I have elaborated on this contradiction in other of my writings and will not burden the present work by repeating this explanation. In any case, no such explanation is necessary if one is going to work on a koan. If you will sit quietly for a few minutes you will become aware of this schism because a tension naturally arises. Normally, we try to do something to get rid of this tension and so calm ourselves. One great self-calming god of our age is television, which enables us to leak away this vital tension. Another much more subtle way to leak away this tension is to practice Zen or some other spiritual way. We can then console ourselves with the thought that if we "work" with the tension, if we concentrate, meditate, or contemplate, the future will in some way be better. However, if we cannot do something, if we cannot lose ourselves in a television program, in a book, or in gossip, if we cannot engage in some spiritual activity, then we feel restless, agitated, and ill at ease.

The doubt sensation comes when we let go of all self-calming devices; but these devices become ever more subtle and difficult to detect as we go deeper into the practice. One after the other we must let go of ways by which we evade the tension, restlessness, and agitation. We can only do this in the light of great faith. In turn, the greater our faith, the greater the doubt we can tolerate. Perhaps doubt is not the most appropriate word because it gives the impression that working with a koan is an intellectual affair, but a koan, as we have said, must engage the whole of our being. Instead of doubt sensation it might be better to call it the dilemma sensation or the double bind.

What is the double bind sensation? It is important to realize each koan has a bite, a twist, that is its entrance point. This bite could be looked on as the double bind. To illustrate what he meant by double bind, Gregory Bateson, who coined the term, used a koan in which the master says, "If you say this is a stick I will punish you; if you say it is not a stick I will punish you." For Bateson the double bind was the result of mutually contradictory commands being given to a person by others in authority with the threat of punishment if both commands were not carried out. It is therefore learned in experience.

The double bind with which we work in koans is inherent, the wound in our being. Experience, existence, and consciousness are born from it. A koan, being a window on to our true self, is also a window on this primary manifestation of our true self. Until we come to full awakening, this double bind, with its accompanying sensation of tension, its feeling of confusion, anguish, and anxiety, and its intellectual nagging, doubting, and questioning, is always present to some degree or other. The ground of our practice is just this confused mass, the *massa confusa* of the alchemists. The masters call it the great doubt.

Perseverance
Shibayama, a contemporary Zen master who died quite recently, said that working with a koan was something like a blind man working his way along the edge of a cliff with the help of a stick. Someone comes along, seizes the stick,

and throws it away, whirls the blind man around three times and throws him to the ground, and then leaves him to find his own way.

In other words, because koans are ways by which we work with the primordial double bind, at first they are not clear and light, but dark and confusing. It is only after working with them for a long while, letting go the erroneous ways that we have used in the past to cope with or to try to escape from the primordial double bind, that they are eventually seen as windows rather than impenetrable walls. Hakuin refers to them as "those vile koans," and Joshu, when someone asked him about the Way, said, "It is bitter." In the Christian tradition this bitter way is given form in a well-known book, *The Dark Night of the Soul,* by St. John of the Cross. Whoever has worked on koans knows well this dark night, this long expanse of dry and discouraging inner terrain that Gurdjieff likened to the Gobi desert. In the Sermon on the Mount, Jesus says, "Blessed are they that hunger and thirst after righteousness." It is only those who do indeed so hunger and thirst who can undertake this pilgrimage to the center of their being across the waste land of a tormented soul.

A dialogue between a visitor and the great contemporary Hindu teacher Nisargadatta sheds light on working with koans, even though it is very unlikely Nisargadatta knew anything about koans or, quite likely, anything about Zen. Nisargadatta had spoken of himself as being "immutable," and the visitor asked "How can I know what immutable means directly and not, as I do, through its dictionary meaning."

Nisargadatta replied, "The word itself is the bridge. Remember it, think of it, explore it, go round it, look at it from all directions, dive into it with earnest perseverance: endure all delays and disappointments, till suddenly the mind turns around, away from the word, towards the reality beyond the word. It is like trying to find a person knowing his name only. . . . The task seems hopeless until suddenly all becomes clear and simple, so wonderfully easy. But as long as you are interested in your present way of living you will shirk from the final leap into the unknown."[2]

Different Kinds of Koans

Every koan expresses true nature, what we have called presence or knowing without the sheaths of knowledge. Sometimes it expresses knowing as emptiness, limitless and boundless. For example, in the first koan of the *Hekiganroku,* Emperor Wu asked Bodhidharma, "What is your teaching?" Bodhidharma replied, "Vast emptiness and nothing that can be called holy." At other times the koan expresses knowing as oneness. For example, a monk asked Joshu, "What is Buddha?" Joshu answered, "The oak tree in the garden." Sometimes, as in koan 11, in which Joshu examines the two hermits, it is expressing not-twoness, and at others, as in the case of koan 19, which we have been talking about, it expresses interpenetration. Some koans fit into more than one of these categories, some fit into all, and of course some do not fit into any of them. Emptiness, oneness, not-twoness, perfect interpenetration, these are all modes of mind at play. (The reader who is interested in following up on this is advised to read *The Four Wisdoms of Hakuin,* in *The Original Face: An Anthology of Rinzai Zen,* edited by Thomas Cleary.) In this regard Buddha on one occasion used the analogy of milk which is now butter, now cheese, now yogurt, but always milk.

---

[2] *I Am That: Talks with Sri Nisargadatta Maharaj.* Tr. Maurice Frydman (Durham: Acorn Press, 1973).

Introduction

A verse written by Layman P'ang, a very famous Zen Buddhist of eighth-century China, together with another koan sums up very well what we have just been saying.

> *Empty-handed I carry the hoe.*
> *Walking I ride the water buffalo.*
> *Crossing the bridge and lo!*
> *The bridge moves while the river stands still.*
> *On top of Mount Fuji a cloud cooks rice.*

Each of these statements is used as a koan, the last being added from another source.

The Essence and the Function

Sometimes koans express presence as essence, sometimes as action. For example, a master and monk were hoeing the garden. The monk asked the master, "What is it?" The master straightened up and stuck his hoe into the ground. The monk said, "You have the essence but you miss the function." The master responded, "All right, what is it?" The monk went on hoeing the ground. The master said, "You have the function but you miss the essence." A very good example of this kind of koan is number 48 in which both essence and function are expressed.

The Breakthrough Koans

Koans can be divided into breakthrough koans and subsequent koans. Working with breakthrough koans one comes to awakening, or *kensho* as it is called in Japan. With kensho one truly sees from the very beginning all beings are Buddha, all are already the awakened one. We must repeat, however, that this does not mean that if you work diligently on the koan you will eventually come to awakening. It means rather that *because you are already Buddha, you eventually see how the koan expresses this truth.* This is what is meant by seeing into a koan. Joshu's Mu!, the Sound of One Hand Clapping, and What Is Your Face Before Your Parents Were Born? are all breakthrough koans; so is the question "who am I?" or "who is the master?" Some people see into these koans in a matter of weeks or months, others take years. A Catholic priest spent forty years working on the koan Mu! Mumon, the master who compiled the *Mumonkan,* worked on Mu! for six years. Let it be repeated, however, one who sees into a koan quickly is not necessarily an advanced person and one who takes a long while is not retarded. Each of us is a complete meal. Each is unique, no difference can be found. From the beginning all beings are Buddha.

We must consider a koan from the point of view of the spiritual maturity of the protagonists. Invariably a monk asks a master a question. We must ask ourselves, is the monk a beginner, has he already seen deeply into the truth of his own being, or has he simply had a brief kensho? Look at each koan from these different perspectives. Look at the response given by the master and suppose it to have been given by a novice, and then ask yourself what would be the difference if such a response were given by a novice or by a master, even though they both used the same words?

Some koans take the form of dharma combat or dharma duel. An awakened monk or master will challenge another equally awakened monk by asking a question. Although the question seems innocuous, it is a bait that hides a barb. An unawakened person would seize the bait and be caught by trying to respond at the verbal level on which the question is asked. A master, however, will take the bait but avoid the barb. We will be encountering some dharma duels in the koans that follow.

Nanto Koans
All koans are difficult for those who have not yet seen into their true nature. But even beyond that difficulty, some are more difficult than others. The most difficult are called *nanto* koans.

The Need for Subsequent Koan Practice After Awakening
We must not think that to pass through the barrier of the patriarch means all of one's past karma is swept away in one fell swoop. On the contrary, this happens very, very rarely. Most of us when we first come to awakening see but a glimpse of our true self; only few have the great explosion that Mumon speaks of in his commentary on the first koan. My teacher Yasutani Roshi used to say that if one were in a dark cave in which no light could enter and were to strike a match, this would bring about a qualitative change in the cave. If one were to light a candle from the match, the light would be brighter, but the change would be quantitative, not qualitative. It would be a further quantitative change if one were to shine a flashlight, then a searchlight, then if one were to break open the roof of the cave and let the sunlight pour in. Each time a change would occur but the change would not be radical as is the first flash of light. So it is with awakening. Although the first glimpse of true nature may be feeble, qualitatively it is no different from the full awakening of Buddha. The purpose of working on subsequent koans is to bring more and more intensity of light to bear. It is as though the whole mind becomes more and more

translucent. But the first breakthrough from the opaque darkness of sleep is the beginning of it all.

We should also realize it's understood that it is simply a preference of Mumon's that makes the Joshu's Mu! the first koan in the *Mumonkan*, and therefore makes it a breakthrough koan. Any of the koans could just as well be the first. This means that each time one sees through a koan, another awakening occurs. To see into a koan, that burst of power, that *Aha!* must come out.

The Function of These Commentaries

Because koans are difficult, most teachers give "handles" to their students by which the koans may be, in a fashion, caught hold of. It is not the function of the commentary to give the answers to the koans. Some teachers in Japan, who did not themselves understand koans, insisted their students give rote "answers" to the koans. At the beginning of the century, a monk there became so disenchanted, justifiably, with this kind of abuse that he exposed the answers in a book that has been translated as *The Sound of One Hand*. To publish "answers" to koans in the West, which is so obsessed with answers, can only create more confusion. As is obvious from what we have been saying, koans have no answers, because they are not questions. They are windows on to the human condition, and each of us sees this human condition from his or her own perspective. This does not mean that any old response will do or that one response is as good as another. Each koan is a particular and quite specific perception, although each person will express this perception in his or her own way. One who is awakened will see fairly readily if another is awakened. In the same way, one who has worked on a koan will readily see whether another has truly seen into it or is simply juggling words. Without some "clues," without some way to penetrate the density of the koan, however, few people would be able to work with them. The following are the kinds of commentaries I have given over the years to students. It is hoped that they will be of some value to others in their work.

Mumon's Preface

In Buddhism mind is the foundation, the dharma gate that has no door. If it has no door how do you pass through? Do you not know that nothing that enters by the gate can be a family treasure—whatever has a cause is always subject to change. Just saying this stirs up waves when no wind blows, stabs wounds in healthy flesh. How much more foolish it is to cling to words and phrases of others trying to achieve some understanding. This is like trying to hit the moon with a stick, or scratching a shoe when the foot itches. What do words have to do with the truth?

In the summer of 1228 I, Ekai, was head monk at Ryusho in Toka. Because the monks begged me to teach them, I at last used the koans of the ancient masters as brick-bats with which to batter at the gate and so guide the monks according to their capability and temperament. I wrote down these koans and now they have, more or less on their own, become quite a collection. I have brought together forty-eight of them but have not arranged them in any particular order. The collection is called *The Mumonkan, "The Gateless Barrier."*

If you are brave you will dive right in without being worried about the risk. Eight-armed Nara may try to stop you, but in vain. Even the twenty-eight patriarchs of India and the six patriarchs of China will cower at such bravery and have to beg for their lives. However, if you hesitate, you will be like someone watching a horse gallop by the window. In a twinkling of an eye it has already gone.

Koans

1 Joshu's Mu!

A monk once asked Joshu, "Does a dog have the Buddha Nature?" Joshu answered, "Mu!"

Mumon's Comment

To practice Zen you must pass the barriers set up by the patriarchs. To know the subtlety of true awakening you must let go of your ordinary, habitual ways of thought. If you do not pass these barriers and do not let go of habitual ways of thought, you are like a ghost clinging to grasses and weeds. Now, what is the barrier of the patriarchs? It is simply mu! Mu! is the main gate of Zen and this is why it is called the "gateless barrier of the Zen tradition."

If you pass through not only will you see Joshu face to face but you will also go hand in hand with the whole line of masters and be in intimate communion with them, seeing everything with the same eyes and hearing everything with the same ears. How wonderful! Who would not want to pass this barrier?

Koans: One

Arouse your entire body with its three hundred and sixty bones and its eighty-four thousand pores; summon up a great mass of doubt and pour it into this question day and night without ceasing. Question it day and night.

Do not take it as nothingness, or as a relative no of "yes and no," "is and is not." It is like swallowing a red hot iron ball; you try to spit it out but cannot.

All the delusive and useless knowledge that you have collected up to the present—throw it away. After a period of time this striving will come to fruition naturally, spontaneously giving way to a condition of internal and external unity. You will know this, but for yourself only, like a dumb person who has had a dream.

Then suddenly it will all give way in an explosion and you will astonish the heavens and shake the earth. It will be as if you have seized the great sword of Kan-u. If you meet the Buddha, you kill the Buddha; when you meet the patriarchs and masters, you will kill the patriarchs and masters. On the brink of life and death you have the great freedom. In the four modes of existence of the six rebirths you enjoy a samadhi of innocent delight

Once more how are you to concentrate on this mu? Every ounce of energy you have must be expended on it; and if you do not give up on the way another lamp of the law will be lit.

Mumon's Verse

The dog! Buddha-nature!
The perfect manifestation, the command of truth.
If for a moment you fall into relativity,
You are dead as a doornail.

Comment

To work on this koan one must *be* the monk asking the question. So we must be sure we know what kind of question he is asking? Is it about doctrine? Does the first monk want to confirm that indeed the dog does have the Buddha nature? Buddhist teaching is that all beings are Buddha. Is the monk concerned about the dog, or about Buddhist theories about dogs? Mumon worked on this koan for six years. He would hit his head against a pillar in the zendo (meditation hall) when he felt drowsy or his mind wandered too much. He and thousands upon thousands of others have struggled and wept for long hours trying to resolve the koan. It is hardly likely that he or they would have worked so hard for just a theory.

In a way this is a tragic koan, calling up, as it does, the anguish of humanity's most haunting questions. Is there life after death? Is there a meaning to my life? Am I all alone in a world that cares nothing for me? Therefore each of us must be the monk because at heart each of us already is the monk. We all have this feeling of vulnerability in the face of sickness, old age, and death, a feeling of fundamental insecurity which, although it may be buried under work, hidden by projects and goals, ignored in the rush of existence, is never absent. In a way the whole human race is blessed and cursed at the same time. We all hunger for our true home, and this hunger, if we heed it, can lead us there, but only across the desert of confusion, doubt, and dismay; this is the curse, because the first thing we encounter on our way home is our own insecurity. If, however, someone is unable to heed the call, is not aware of a longing for perfection, a yearning for unconditional love, a conviction of something, some other way of being, some happiness or peace that

passes all understanding, and if that person is not prepared
to pay the price of wandering in the desert of insecurity and
anguish, then Zen is not for him or her.

Most often, before I give this or any other breakthrough koan to students, I have them spend some time asking themselves, "What is my fundamental question, what is
of utmost concern to me?" Sometimes I say, "Imagine you
have the wisest person possible in front of you, Buddha,
Jesus, even God, and you have but one question you can
ask. What would your question be?" Sometimes they ask,
"What is the meaning of my life?" or "What is a good life?"
or, more often, "Why must I and others suffer so much?" or
"What is death and why do I have to die?" But I press them
and say, "Is this really your question?" Very often, after
some prompting they will say, "No, but it is the nearest I
can get to what is the real question." What T.S. Eliot calls
the overwhelming question cannot really be put into words,
it is an ache tinged with dread, a bewilderment mixed with a
feeling of the injustice of the situation, a wishing, a longing,
an "I don't know what."

We have to see the monk as wandering in the wilder-
ness of doubt and confusion. He hears of a Zen master
reputed to be wise and compassionate, and decides to visit
him. All the monk's yearning and fears come to the surface.
As a human being he is vulnerable, fragile, facing certain
death at an uncertain time, threatened with sickness, and
inexorably going toward old age. He has been told that all
beings are Buddha, they are whole and complete, but this
has no reality for him. He decides to ask the Zen master for
reassurance; this will give him something to hold on to,
something secure in the stormy ocean of insecurity. And so
he asks whether a dog has Buddha nature. A dog at that

time was at about the level of a rat in our own time. It was the lowest of the low. The implication is that if a dog has Buddha nature then I too must have Buddha nature. If it has Buddha nature then I am saved, I have a life saver to support me in the storms of life.

And Joshu says, "No!"

This koan has a counterpart in koan 29 of a collection called the *Hekiganroku*. A monk asks the Zen master Daizui, "At the time of the great conflagration does 'it' go too?" Buddhist cosmology says that at the end of an eon the world is destroyed by a great conflagration and the monk is asking whether, at this time, "it," Buddha nature or true nature is also destroyed. The master says, "Yes! It goes too." The monk doesn't quite know what to say and stammers, still hoping, "So it will go with the rest?" And the master, without mercy, agrees, "It will be gone with the rest." Again one has to imagine the monk anxiously asking this question; better still one must *be* the monk anxiously asking this question. Does anything survive death? Is anything permanent, indestructible? We are told a human being is Buddha nature, or, if one prefers, a spirit. At the time of the great conflagration, at the time of Armageddon, the Buddha nature, the spirit, does it go too?

The master says yes! it goes too, it will go with the rest.

Most people have bouts of anxiety or depression. Some also have had an all too fleeting taste of what it means to be whole and complete, and, when faced with the confusion, conflicts, and complexities of life, they have a sense of the unreality, even of the absurdity of the human condition that goes far beyond anxiety. Because of the anxiety, the unreality, the absurdity, so it is said, we all need something or someone on whom we can rely. Once upon a time it was the priest, nowadays it is the doctor or psychiatrist, or even Ann Landers. We look for someone we feel can give support, succor, and spiritual nourishment in these times of dread. The monk felt Joshu was such a one. Joshu was over eighty at the time, and from about age eighteen had worked on himself under the guidance of Nansen, and then after Nansen's death went on pilgrimage for twenty long years. He was one of the great masters of the time. No wonder the monk turned to him, full of hope and expectation.

But then Joshu says, "Mu!"

I remember a similar occasion when I was a younger man. Troubled by the fear of death, feeling the meaninglessness of my life, desperate for some help, I went to see a priest who was recommended to me by the family doctor. I told my fears and longings to the priest and he advised me, "Young man, you are trying to find the impossible. My advice to you is to look after your wife and family, forget all about all this, get yourself a television, and live without all this worry about things no human being can ever understand. This is the sort of thing you should leave to the saints." I was crushed.

Was Joshu as lost as this priest?

Here is the bite of the koan, the contradiction. The practice of Zen is the practice of wisdom and compassion. With wisdom comes responsiveness, flexibility, and sensitivity to the situation. With compassion comes the need and ability to share with others in their suffering, to wish ardently to find some way to relieve others of their burden. Not only this, but Buddhist teaching is that all beings are Buddha. Thus on both accounts, as a wise and compassionate man, and as one well versed in Buddhist doctrine, why does Joshu say "No!"? This answer is like snatching a crust of bread from the grasp of a starving man. The monk, like a blind man, is feeling his way along the edge of a precipice of insecurity and Joshu whirls him around and throws him to the ground after depriving him of his last means of support. Why does Joshu do this? Why does a wise, compassionate, and knowledgeable man take away the last hope of a monk in distress?

The same question must be asked of Daizui. He must have known that Buddhist doctrine specifically states that "it" cannot be destroyed, even by the great conflagration. Furthermore, in the verse that Etcho wrote about this latter koan it is said,

> Blocked by a double barrier,
> The monk asked from the heart of the kalpa fire.

That the monk asked "from the heart of the kalpa fire" means he was burning in the fires of purgatory. Out of this burning came the question, "Is there something above, beyond, outside of this terrible anxiety, something that cannot be burned up in the fires of purgatory?" Why did Daizui not soothe him, not give him balm?

Mumon points to the answer when, in his commentary, he warns that you must cut off ordinary ways of thought, because if you don't "then you will be like a ghost clinging to grasses and weeds." A ghost is without substance, the grasses and weeds are worn out phrases and beliefs. Beliefs in God, in Buddha, in an afterlife, in a heaven or pure land, as well as in nothing, annihilation, nothing after death, are just and only that, *beliefs*. The belief that we need something to hold on to when the going gets rough is itself a belief and untrue. The belief that we can ignore these questions, that we can simply get on with the business of living, is also untrue. It is precisely *because* we cling to something, even if that something is negation, that the going does get rough. By clinging to the weeds, by building up idols with words and phrases, we turn our back on our own true nature that is not dependent on affirmation, belief, or the blessings of any master or priest. This is why Mumon says that after you have seen into your true nature, "If you meet the Buddha, you kill the Buddha; when you meet the patriarchs and masters, you will kill the patriarchs and masters." To kill is to purge one's mind of Buddha, of Jesus, of any and all kinds of saviors. Mumon goes on, "On the brink of life and death you have the great freedom." Notice that where formerly great anxiety burned now all is at peace.

Mu is the main gate of Zen, it is the royal entrance, and yet, as Mumon says, it is the barrier of the patriarchs. Our conscious mind turns everything upside down. In place of untrammeled freedom, the mind makes a frozen wasteland; instead of immutability, the mind creates great agitation; whereas each one of us is reality itself, the mind confers this reality upon illusions and makes of us ghosts in the weeds. Consciousness is a stage on which the drama of life and death is enacted, but it is also a barrier to the truth. But we can pass through this barrier, we can walk through the wall of the mind. We need not be deterred by the "trespassers will be prosecuted" notices that litter the mind. And when we do pass through we are one with the intelligence that is Buddha, Joshu, the patriarchs, and the long line of masters. This means we are one also with the intelligence that is the poor, miserable dog slinking along, muddy, moth-eaten, and lost.

But to do this we must work with all our heart and

with all our soul. As Mumon tells us, we must work with the entire body, "with its three hundred and sixty bones and its eighty-four thousand pores." We must "summon up a great mass of doubt and pour it into this question day and night without ceasing. Question it day and night." One does this anyway. One is always questioning in this way. We are always filled with a great mass of doubt. We call it stress or confusion or worry, but, fundamentally, we are always face to face with this one overwhelming question. The trouble is that we try to respond to the question in the wrong way. We look to success, or to the love of another, to possessions, to knowledge, to goodness to resolve our insecurity. *We look outside ourselves.* We look for *something.* Every desire we have is the desire for oneness, for wholeness. The problem is we try to pin oneness down, we try to make something of it and we suffer the frustration of failure.

Hakuin says in his famous "Chant in Praise of Zazen," "If we turn inward and prove our true nature/That true self is no-self our own self is no-self." This is seeing into Mu! It is seeing our original face before our parents were born. *True self is no self.* To see this is to pass the barrier of the patriarchs.

Basho says in one of his haiku [a seventeen-syllable poem]:

No one walks along this path
This autumn evening.

When working with Mu! one must ask who is this no one? What is this no self? But heed Mumon's warning: "Do not take it as nothingness, nor as a relative no of 'yes and no,' 'is and is not.'" It is not negation. It is "like swallowing a red hot iron ball; you try to spit it out but cannot."

Koans: One

Hakuin too says something similar when he describes it as a rat in a bamboo tube that cannot go forward, cannot go back, but cannot stay where it is. One is damned if one does, damned if one doesn't, forever caught in the primordial double bind. We try to use all our previous strategies and methods. We try to cheat, seduce; we get angry, indulge in self-pity. We try to use logic, reason, we read scriptures, we attend seminars. We fret and fume. But, as Mumon declares, we must eventually throw away all the delusive and useless knowledge that we have collected up to the present. Then, after a period of time, this striving will come to fruition naturally, spontaneously giving way to a condition of internal and external unity.

Those who have not practiced with koans do not understand this striving. They think that the striving is to *attain* something. At first, of course, it is. To attain something, to be something, to know something are the principle strategies we use when faced with the primordial double bind. *But this is only at first.* When at last we have exhausted all the resources of our being and have let go of all the delusive and useless knowledge, then the striving is quite different. It is more of a yearning to be at one with a beloved, a yearning that finally becomes its own consummation.

"Suddenly," as Mumon describes it, "it will all give way in an explosion and you will astonish the heavens and shake the earth." How can one describe such an explosion? What joy, what relief. One way of getting a feel for this is as follows. Suppose you are going on a journey and you have looked forward to it for a whole year. The night before you cannot sleep because of excitement. You are all ready. Packed. Waiting for the taxi. And then someone asks, "Do you have your tickets?" Tickets, where are the tickets? They are not in your purse. They are not in your pocket. Where are the tickets? You run into the bedroom. Did you leave them on the table? No, they are not there. The taxi sounds its horn. But where are the tickets? They must be in the living room. You run into the living room. No, they are not there. Oh! what have you done with them? Again the taxi. You feel like weeping in desperation. You'll be late for the plane. Perhaps, who knows, they won't let you on without tickets. You run back into the bedroom again—no, not there. Back into the living room. Search through your purse. Empty your pockets. The taxi driver comes in. "Are you ready?" You hate the taxi driver. "I can't find the tickets! I've lost the tickets! Oh! what will I do?" The taxi driver strides over to the small table and picks up the novel that you are taking on the plane with you. Pulls out an envelope. "Is this what you are looking for?" Wow! the tickets, the lovely tickets. Oh, what a wonderful taxi driver, what a wonderful world, what a wonderful moment! In that explosion of finding, the world is turned upside down. What joy, what relief. But the tickets were never lost. They were always there, waiting patiently until you stopped running around and picked up the book.

> At last I've broken Unmon's barrier,
> There's exit everywhere—East, West, North, South,
> In at morning, out at evening neither host nor guest.
> My every step stirs up a little breeze.

—A satori poem by Daito (1282-1337)

35

2 Hyakujo's Fox

Whenever Master Hyakujo delivered a sermon, an old man was always there listening with the monks. When they left he left too. One day, however, he remained behind. The master asked him, "Who are you standing in front of me?" The old man replied, "I am not a human being. In the past, in the time of Kashyapa Buddha, I lived on the mountain as a Zen priest. On one occasion a monk asked me, 'Is an awakened person subject to the law of causation or not?' I answered, 'He is not.' Because of this answer I have had to live as a fox for five hundred lives. Now, I beg you, Master, please say a turning word on my behalf and release me from the fox's body." Then he asked, "Is an awakened person subject to the law of causation or not?" The master answered, "No one can escape the law of karma." As soon as he heard this the old *man was awakened. Bowing, he said, "I have now been released from the fox's body, which can be found behind the mountain. May I make a request of the master? Please perform a funeral ceremony for me as you would for a dead priest."*

The master had the head monk strike the gavel and announce to the rest that after the meal a funeral service would be held for a dead priest. The monks wondered, musing, "We are all healthy. No one is sick in the infirmary. What is going on?" After the meal, the master led the monks and, with his staff, from under a bush he poked out the body of a dead fox. He then performed the ceremony of cremation.

That evening the master ascended the rostrum in the hall and told the monks the whole story. Obaku, a senior disciple, thereupon asked, "The man of old missed the turning word and had to live as a fox for five hundred lives. Suppose every time he answered he had made no mistakes, what would have happened then?" The master responded, "Just come here a moment and I'll tell you." Obaku went up to the master and slapped him. The master clapped his hands and, laughing aloud, cried, "I thought the barbarian's beard was red, but here is a red-bearded barbarian."

Mumon's Comment

"Not subject to the law of causation"—why did he have to live out his lives as a fox? "No one can escape the law of karma"—for what reason was he released from the body of a fox? If with regard to this you have the one eye, then you will understand that the former Hyakujo enjoyed his five hundred lives as a fox.

Koans: Two

Mumon's Verse

Not falling, not escaping,
Two faces, one die.
Not escaping, not falling
A thousand mistakes, ten thousand mistakes.

Comment

"I am not a human being." This second koan is acted out against the background of this affirmation. You, the reader, are not a human being either. You are not a man or a woman, you are not a Canadian, American, English, French, or Japanese person. Indeed, you are not a person at all. Neither are you a body or brain, not a soul, spirit, nor even Buddha nature. And you are most certainly not nothing. But please resist the temptation to ask, "Then what am I?" This lust to be something is the cause of all karma. We ask little children, "What will you be when you grow up?" Furthermore, do we not call out when tormented by fate, tormented by others, "Oh! Please just let me be!" Psychologist Erik Erikson said that the search for identity, to know what one is finally and for all time, is a basic motivation of human beings. Titles, grades, degrees, classes, medals, uniforms, certificates, diplomas, names, graduation ceremonies, initiation ceremonies, taking the vows of monks, of priests, the ways and means for establishing an identity, for "knowing who I am," are endless.

If you have heard the sound of one hand clapping, have passed through the barrier of mu, you will know what it means to be able to say "I am not a human being." If you have not broken through, to hear that statement is mystifying, and you might be tempted to believe the old man is just playing with words. On the contrary, awakening to the faith mind by which one enters into the vast mystery of knowing and being comes when you see clearly you are not a human being. Furthermore, one works to resolve koans by way of the faith mind. Before penetrating the first koan we wander around lost in the darkness, and then suddenly clarity bursts in. Knowing is freed from the bondage of knowledge, being is freed from the bondage of things, and "I am" is freed from the curse of having to be something. I am not a human being.

Zen is part of the Mahayana school of Buddhism. The other school is the Theravada or Hinayana. In actual fact the word Hinayana is often used in a pejorative way and then means one works simply for one's own salvation. As such it is unfair to equate Hinayana with the Theravada on the one hand and Mahayana with Zen on the other. Many people practice Zen as Hinayanists, and many Theravadins practice as Mahayanists. Indeed, all of us probably start as Hinayanists. The ideal of the Hinayanists is the Arhat, the one who is freed from the wheel of birth and death and is no longer subject to past karma and, being no longer liable to rebirth, retires to eternal rest. This is the significance of Obaku's question, "The man of old missed the turning word and fell to the state of a fox for five hundred lives. Suppose every time he answered he made no mistakes, what would happen then?" No mistake, no error, and, ultimately, no sin. What happens if a person life after life commits no sin?

On the other hand, the idea of the Mahayanist Buddhist is the Bodhisattva. In a Buddhist sutra it says, "Just so the Bodhisattva, when he comprehends the dharma as he should, does not retire into *Blessed Rest*. In wisdom then he dwells." The Sanskrit word for Blessed Rest is *nirvrti,* meaning "Nirvana which excludes the world of suffering."

We have to see the difference between these two alternative ways of gaining freedom, the Hinayanist and the Mahayanist, as a basic theme of this koan.

We may prefer to change a little the wording of the question put to the old man, and instead of asking whether or not an awakened person is subject to the law of causation, we might want to know if it is possible to find a way out of the rat race of frustration and confusion we call life. In Christianity we are promised heaven, the Muslims are promised paradise, the Buddhists of the pure land school are promised "the pure land." Call it what you will, these religions are promising personal salvation, a way out of the rat race. The promise can be fulfilled only after we are dead, so we have no way of really knowing for certain, at least as far as others are concerned, if it is kept or not. But even so, in the past, most people believed in some kind of heaven. Nowadays we are all more skeptical and pessimistic, we tend to see death as an end, annihilation, nothing. But even in this nothing persists the optimistic belief that a way out of the rat race is possible. Rest in peace is the wish we have for all the dead and departed.

This is the Hinayanist's way. The way out is by climbing the scale of samadhi, purifying the mind more and more until eventually one is no longer bound down and can step out of the rat race. In Obaku's words, every time one is asked a question one gives the right answer. But the heart of the koan is the Mahayanist's response.

The old man says, Yes, there is a possible way out of the rat race, so he is punished by having to live for five hundred lives as a fox. In the West we talk about people being cunning as a fox. The word *cunning* comes from an old English word that means to "know all." When working on this koan I was told that in the East this is not the case. Instead of knowing all, people there look upon the fox as knowing but half the truth. However, it is still possible to know all even though one only knows half, and it is possible that one only knows half when one knows all. You have probably seen the ambiguous picture of a vase and two faces. When you see the one, the vase, you do not see the other, the two faces. However, when you see the vase you see all, you know all that can be known about the vase, even though you only know half of the picture.

But apart from all this, why was the old man punished for saying the awakened person is not subject to the law of causation? After all he is only telling us what we would expect. Is this not what spiritual practice is about? Do we not practice a spiritual path to free ourselves from the trammels of existence, to find peace and love, to get off the gerbil wheel of samsara?

Koan 1 of the *Hekiganroku* gives an interesting parallel to the present case. It is about a visit of Bodhidharma, the first Chinese patriarch of Zen, to Emperor Wu of China, who had done a great deal for the development of Buddhism in that country. He had been a "good" man, and being human, he asked, "What is my reward for all of the good that I have done?" Bodhidharma replies, "No reward at all, Sire!" Many a person, after practicing Zen Buddhism for a month, six months, a year, six years, moans "What am I getting out of this sweat and pain?" Nothing, Bodhidharma would say.

What has this nothing to do with our koan? One basic question the koan is concerned with is whether we have to bear the consequences of our actions, or can escape them. If we do have to pay for our faults and the old man, therefore, was punished justly, should we not, as did Emperor Wu, expect to be rewarded for our virtues and gather the fruit of our good actions?

Let us say we do have to bear the consequences of our actions. Then why does Bodhidharma say no merit, no reward? If Bodhidharma is right and the law of karma does not apply as far the emperor was concerned and he gains no merit for his good actions, why was the old man who listened to Hyakujo punished? After all, in his own way he was only giving the same kind of reply as Bodhidharma. He had to live for five hundred years as a fox; should not Bodhidharma have said that the emperor would go to heaven?

It is a sad thing that many people who have practiced Zen for a long while, even some who teach Zen, have not come to terms with this koan. One American teacher has even gone so far as to say that Buddhism has nothing to do with ethics and morality. One of the things that puzzles many people is the admonition of Zen to get beyond good and evil. To get beyond good and evil seems to imply to get beyond morality and ethics, to escape the law of karma. It is this mistake that the American teacher is making. Unfortunately, these people take their spurious teaching into life and violate the precepts in the belief they are beyond "all of that." They end up miserable or with some evil karma of unacceptable behavior, all the while pleading that because they are "enlightened" they are no longer subject even to the rules of decency.

The koan is about the nature of the awakened state and karma. Is awakening simply one's own personal salvation, or is it something much more subtle, indeed something that it is impossible to grasp by the conscious mind with its intellectual structures and verbal containers? What is the connection between awakening and karma? What is the merit for coming to awakening?

Basically, the koan is about the meaning of "I am not a human being." If an awakened person is not subject to the law of karma, then, because we are all inherently fully awakened, none of us is. But how can this be possible? How can it be said we are all free of the law of karma?

Quite obviously it cannot be said because Hyakujo affirms, "No one can escape the law of karma." However, and this must not be missed, it is on hearing this that the old man is awakened. When he hears Hyakujo's statement, "No one can escape the law of karma," he escapes the law of karma! He is finally released from the fox's body. As Mumon asks in his commentary, how is this possible? He asks how it is that when the old man says, "Not subject to the law of causation" he had to live out his lives as a fox? Yet when Hyakujo said that no one can escape the law of karma the old man was released from the body of a fox?

This is the bite of the koan: put in full it is "I am not a human being, yet as a human being I am subject to the law of karma." Let us be quite clear, we must not assume the old man gave the wrong answer and Hyakujo gave the right one. Nor should we believe Hyakujo's answer in some way cancels out the old man's, as when a plus cancels out a minus. Nor must we think, as some teachers teach, that by simply being one with the fox, one with the whole world, including the church bell striking midnight, we have resolved the whole dilemma, because by doing this, by entering into a samadhi state, and simply being one with all, we have taken the route of the Hinayanists.

We must see into the koan.

In his verse Mumon presses the same question:

Koans: Two

Not falling, not escaping,
Two faces, one die.
Not escaping, not falling
A thousand mistakes, ten thousand mistakes.

In the tradition in which I was taught, after we had passed through the koans of the *Mumonkan* and the *Hekiganroku*, we were required to tackle the ten Buddhist precepts, considering each one as a koan. We had to see each precept from different points of view, first, from the point of view of the Hinayanist, then from that of the Mahayanist, then from the point of view of three other levels, each calling for a more and more subtle interpretation.

For example, the first precept is, "Not to kill, but to cherish all life." The Hinayanist approach is literal: one just does not kill. Monks following this path would go to the greatest extreme not to kill. They would strain water so they would not inadvertently swallow insects and so kill them, they would wear bells to warn small animals of their approach and so not crush them. Some monks would even walk on stilts to minimize the possibility of killing small living creatures. However, what does a Hinayanist do if a mad dog is about to attack a child? To eat at all, some life must be lost. Creation is almost invariably accompanied by destruction. For the Mahayanist, therefore, the *intention* as the guiding factor instead of the action is what matters. This of course can lend itself to all kinds of sophistry unless a person is serious about following a spiritual path.

The Mahayanist approach is no longer concerned with rules of behavior, or morality as it is more generally called. Instead it is now a question of ethics, which takes the rules of behavior as a guide but imposes an even more stringent demand on the person, the demand that he or she takes responsibility for his or her actions. It is evident that from the point of view of the Hinayanist, it is possible to get off the wheel of samsara because a rule permits, even demands, only yes or no, success or failure, right or wrong. At this level of morality one can live according to a moral code and that is either kept or broken. But at this level how does one deal with the double bind?

For example, an employer runs into hard times. He is faced with possibly having to dismiss a number of employees so he can pay the debts incurred by the business. This, in turn, will mean the company can stay open and so give employment to the employees who remain on the payroll. Or he can decide to keep all the employees and run the risk of going bankrupt, causing all to lose their jobs. What must he do? Assuming that he is sensitive to others and aware of his responsibility toward them, he is damned if he does and he is damned if he doesn't. No rules of behavior are of any help. Whatever action he chooses he will sacrifice the good to do good, and therefore whatever he does will be a burden, whatever he does will create karma. As Shakespeare says in *Julius Caesar*, "The evil that men do lives after them/The good is oft interr'd with their bones."

We said the precepts can be looked at from three higher levels. Possibly the highest level is the level of one mind, of "I am not a human being." At this level one must ask, who is the person responsible for keeping the rules? Who is it that suffers the punishment for failing to keep the rules? This level has even more stringent demands because one must truly love one's neighbor, as oneself, and *any* act of separation is a violation of the first precept, *any* act of separation is an act of killing. As it is said in Zen, "A tenth of an

inch is all the difference between heaven and hell." In sepa-
rating ourselves from others we separate ourselves from ourselves, and we die to the life of wholeness and are reborn to
the life of division and suffering, to the life of karma. Can
you see why Mumon would have said in his commentary,
"If with regard to this you have the one eye, then you will
understand that the former Hyakujo enjoyed his five hundred lives as a fox"? The one eye is the highest level from
which we can look at the precepts.

Let us not forget, however, that simply because one
has had a glimpse of this truth "I am beyond all form," it
does not mean that one can live in accordance with this
glimpse. In Buddhism it is said "One ordinary thought and
Buddha is an ordinary person. One enlightened thought and
the ordinary person is Buddha." To live a life of no separation is beyond most of us. This koan is an invitation to an
ethical life, a life that is thoroughly grounded in a moral life.
Although one gets beyond good and bad, one does not
thereby obtain a license to commit evil.

Let us return now to the koan. Obaku asks, "The man
of old missed the turning word and had to live out five hundred lives as a fox. Suppose every time he answered he made
no mistakes, what would happen then?" This as we have
already seen is a clever question because it sums up the
whole mystery of the awakened state: what do fully awakened persons do after they reach full awakening? Is it simply
a question of vanishing into nothing? This is what the koan
is about. It is made vividly alive by the master saying, "Just
come here a moment and I'll tell you," and Obaku going up
to the master and slapping him. Obaku beat Hyakujo to it,
Hyakujo was obviously going to whack Obaku for asking a
question. But why did Obaku deserve a beating, and if he

didn't deserve a beating, was he not wrong in beating Hyakujo? And if he did do wrong in beating Hyakujo, did he not deserve a beating? The master clapped his hands and, laughing aloud, said, "I thought the barbarian's beard was red, but here is a red-bearded barbarian."

The rat race, the treadmill of existence, the wheel of samsara, "I thought the barbarian's beard was red, but here is a red-bearded barbarian" This is what the koan is about. But, as Mumon observed, the old man must have enjoyed his five hundred lives as a fox. Someone asked Nansen, "What will you be after you are dead?" Nansen said, "A water buffalo."

I am not a human being.

3 Gutei's Finger

*W*henever he was asked a question, Gutei simply raised his finger. One day a visitor asked Gutei's attendant, "What is your master's teaching?" The boy too raised a finger. Hearing about this, Gutei cut off the boy's finger with a knife. The boy, screaming with pain, started to run away. Suddenly Gutei called to him, and when the boy turned around, Gutei raised a finger. The boy came suddenly to awakening.

When Gutei was about to die he said to the assembled monks, "I got one-finger Zen from Tenryu and used it all my life, but could not exhaust it."

Mumon's Comment

The awakenings of Gutei and the boy are not in the finger. If you really see through this, Tenryu, Gutei, the boy, and you yourself are all run through with one skewer.

Gutei's Finger

Mumon's Verse

> Gutei made a fool of old Tenryu,
> With a sharp knife he freed the boy.
> Korei raised his hand and, with no effort,
> The great ridge of Mount Ka was split in two!

Comment

This koan is very popular and appears in the *Mumonkan,* the *Hekiganroku,* (number 19) and also the *Book of Serenity* (number 84). In the latter two versions the koan simply reads, "Whenever Gutei was asked a question, he simply raised a finger." However, Mumon had mercy on those who were to work with the koan and added the extra part about the attendant. Indeed, the crux of Mumon's koan is when the boy turned to Gutei after his finger had been cut off and Gutei raised a finger. What did the boy see in that finger that brought him to awakening? Or, what is virtually the same question in different words, when in the future the boy was asked a similar question, how would he respond?

The koan starts off, "Whenever Gutei was asked a question. . . ." One should not interpret this biographically, but rather ask what does it mean, "*Whenever* he was asked a question. . . ." It could say "*Invariably* when he was asked a question," or "Without fail," or "always." Why this constancy? "Is there a life after death?" Gutei raises a finger, "Is there a meaning to my life?" Gutei raises a finger. "Am I all alone in a world that cares nothing for me?" Gutei raises a finger. Always the same response.

Some people say that Gutei's finger stands for one mind, a symbol for unity. This was the boy's mistake. In Zen one is admonished not to confuse the finger with the moon to which it points. But then, what does the moon point to? Zen patriarch Fa Yen was asked, "What is the moon?" and he replied, "The finger." He was then asked, "What is the finger?" and he replied, "The moon."

In an earlier commentary we said that words hold, as it were, the truth at arm's length. But this is not possible. Words are the truth just as gestures are. Why should raising the finger be any nearer the truth than saying, "One mind"? It is for this reason that Fa Yen says, "The moon" in response to "What is the finger?" But it is only when we can see into this koan that we realize the finger is the moon. Until then even the moon is but the finger.

In a previous koan, Obaku said the old man failed to give "the turning word." What is the turning word? Gutei too on one occasion failed to give a turning word. He was living as a hermit far from civilization, practicing zazen very seriously. One evening a nun happened to pass by. Gutei invited her to have a meal with him and stay the night and the nun agreed, "I'll do so if you can give me a word of Zen." In Zen literature one often meets with nuns and old ladies who completely stump Zen monks and masters. We will meet a few during our journey through the *Mumonkan*. The nun's question seems a very innocent one: one comes up against it every now and again when someone asks, "Tell me, what exactly is Zen?" Doing zazen, working on koans, following the breath, seeing into one's true nature. Yes, it is all that, but we still haven't really got to the Zen part. What is Zen? Sometimes the question is, "Why did Bodhidharma come from the West?" So this nun asks Gutei, "Give me a word of Zen." What is a word that is not the finger but the moon? And Gutei did not know what to say or do. Coming to this point of not knowing what to say is crucial in Zen. It's like reaching the end of the road while the journey still goes on.

The nun got up and left.

Now this was a very courageous act on her part and underlines the seriousness of Gutei's failure. She was not likely to come across shelter again that night because Gutei had established his hermitage far from others. It also probably meant she would not eat either, and therefore, for her to leave was a double failure on the part of Gutei.

Gutei was filled with remorse and felt his Zen practice had been a waste of time. He must have anguished, "How is it possible that I am unable to give an adequate response?" He vowed to leave his hermitage, but before he could do so he had a dream in which he was told to remain where he was because a Zen master would visit him in the very near future. In a few days the master Tenryu came by. Still filled with remorse and doubt Gutei asked Tenryu, "What is a word of Zen?" Tenryu raised a finger. At this moment Gutei came to awakening. As Mumon says in the koan, "When Gutei was about to die he said to his assembled monks, 'I got one-finger Zen from Tenryu and used it all my life but could not exhaust it.' "

Now the question is why was it all right for Gutei to get one-finger Zen from Tenryu, but not for the attendant to get it from Gutei? A similar question is raised with regard to Bodhidharma. During the interview he had with the emperor, Wu asked him "What are you?" Bodhidharma replied, "I don't know." Later, after Bodhidharma had left, a courtier asked the emperor, "Do you know who that man was, my lord?" The emperor answered, "I don't know." Both Wu and Bodhidharma say, "I don't know." But is "I don't know" the same for both men?

Once again Mumon steps in to help and warns that the satori of Gutei and the boy attendant are not in the finger. We noted earlier that the problem with parables, metaphors, and symbols is that they can do their job so well that we are beguiled into believing that the finger is the moon. Mumon is warning us not to make this confusion. Both Gutei and his attendant in their own way exhausted all the resources of their being. Both were brought to the abyss of their own true nature, and it was only then each could plunge into renewed life by the raising of a finger. Someone observed "If you see into a speck of dust, you see into the whole universe." But, in his introduction to this koan on Gutei's finger in the *Hekiganroku,* Master Setcho asks, "Before the speck of dust is raised, how will you then see into it?" To exhaust all the resources of your being means to cut off all thought, to arrive at the point before the least thought arises. After the boy's finger was cut off, how would he then reply to a question? It is like working on mu. Before the thought of mu arises, what is mu?

After reading Mumon's verse one has to ask, in what way did Gutei make a fool of old Tenryu? How does one make a fool of someone? One way is to take something the person thinks is so and show that it is not so. By cutting off his finger Gutei freed the boy. Yet Tenryu used that finger to reveal the truth. Is this the way that Gutei made a fool of Tenryu?

Although Gutei would raise the finger whenever anyone asked him a question, he only ever raised it once, and then when he did he raised the whole universe.

As it is said in the Gospel of St. Thomas,
When you make the two one,
You will become the sons of man;
If then you say, "Mountain move!"
It will move.

—Robert M. Grant in *The Secret Sayings of Jesus*

4 The Barbarian's Beard

akuan said, "Why has the Western barbarian no beard?"

Mumon's Comment
Practice must be real practice. Awakening must be true awakening. Once you have come face to face with the barbarian, you will have got "it" at last. But by talking about coming face to face, separation has already occurred.

Mumon's Verse

Don't discuss your dream
Before a fool.
Barbarian with no beard
Obscures clarity.

Comment

The Western barbarian is Bodhidharma, who, it is said, came from India or Persia. He has been the subject of numerous sumi paintings, all of which depict him as a swarthy man with beetling brows and a black bushy beard. This beard must have fascinated the Chinese in particular, because as a rule they cannot grow beards, or at least cannot grow the luxuriant growth Bodhidharma was able to produce.

To work on this koan one must see Wakuan, beardless, looking at a picture of Bodhidharma hanging on the wall, and asking himself, "Why has Bodhidharma no beard?" And then one must *become* Wakuan in front of the picture.

We face an obvious contradiction here. The picture on the wall is of Bodhidharma with a bushy beard; and yet Wakuan is wondering why he has no beard. To make things worse Wakuan was an awakened Zen master who would obviously not ask idle or stupid questions. Unfortunately, not much is known about him other than that he wrote an interesting death poem:

The iron tree blossomed,
The cock laid eggs;
Seventy-two years,
The cradle string snaps.

The contradiction is the entrance point of the koan. Wakuan is saying something fundamental about ourselves and our relation to others. He is urging us to go beyond the view we have of ourselves as separate, alienated things or persons in an uncaring and dead world.

However, before getting to the entrance point it might be as well to dwell on the question, "why?" The koan would be quite valid although completely different if Wakuan had simply said, "The Western barbarian has no beard," and we must see into this "why?" It is obviously not put in just to make the koan a more interesting one.

At one Zen center it was said that "why?" simply stirred up the intellectual mind to asking questions beyond its scope and power and therefore was a useless question. It is true enough that in this scientific age we tend to transform "why?" questions into "how?" We do not ask *why* the sun shines, but *how* does it shine. We do not ask why is there life on earth, but seek to understand how life functions. But is there not a place for "why?" even so? Is it possible that sometimes "why?" is not so much calling for information, as expressing something otherwise inexpressible. As any parent knows, children love to ask this question! At the Zen center we just mentioned, young parents were told to do their best to dissuade their children from asking why, in the belief that in this way they could be helped to avoid the pitfall of the intellectual mind becoming the master in their lives. Is it possible, though, that something fundamental could be denied an outlet in this way?

What is the value of the "why?" On the face of it the question does seem to be redundant. Why do birds sing? Why do flowers grow? Why does it rain on the sea? The parents were told to reply to children's questions with the simple "because." Birds sing *because* they sing; flowers bloom *because* they bloom. But is the question redundant? Do we lose anything by banishing "why?" to the outer darkness?

In a way one could say one loses everything. Far from wanting children to stop asking "why?" we should encourage their questions, encourage them to go deeper. But first we should have explored our own source of "why?"

In Zen we speak of the *doubt sensation*, but perhaps we should speak of the *wonder* sensation. I wonder! How few of us do in fact wonder, and how much poorer our lives are because we do not, indeed because we *cannot*, wonder. "I wonder." How wonderful! How full of wonder. In

Shakespeare's *The Tempest* Miranda, who had retained her innocence and so her capacity for wonder, says,

Oh, wonder!
How beauteous mankind is! Oh, brave new world,
That has such people in't.

This is the kind of reaction one has when one first comes to awakening.

All other questions, "what?" "where?" "when?" "how?" all lead to some positive and factual response. All dwell within the realm of the possible. But "why?" takes us out of ourselves. It opens up the mind. A child, at least when first asking the question "why?" is probably experiencing this feeling of wonder to some degree or another. To wonder is to arouse the mind, and if the wonder is deep enough, the mind is totally aroused, without resting on anything.

Let us take another look at the koan. Wakuan is standing there in front of the picture. He is perhaps scratching his head, or rubbing his chin, wondering why that fellow has no beard. Wondering. Just as in the koan of Hyakujo's Fox the phrase "I am not a human being" is the background, so in this koan "why?" is the backdrop.

Why has the barbarian no beard? Again we must not yield to a temptation to make Bodhidharma a symbol for the awakened state and then say that in his awakened state Bodhidharma has no beard, nor has he eyes, ears, nose, tongue, body, or mind. Nor should we look upon the beard as a symbol for defilements that are shed when we attain to our true nature. Although these observations may be true enough in their own way, they are not the point of the koan. They require no leap of faith for their sense to be revealed.

One must ask who is Bodhidharma, or better still, who is the other? A story might help here. Ganto (we will encounter him later) was a celebrated master of a temple that was plundered by brigands. During the robbery one of the villains plunged his sword into Ganto's chest, and as he did this, Ganto let out a great cry and died. When Hakuin heard of this he was filled with misgiving, pondering how an awakened monk could be unable to escape the swords of thieves. Later, after a period of intense meditation, Hakuin came to awakening. He described what happened by saying that he chanced to hear the sound of the temple bell and was suddenly transformed. He said it was as if a sheet of ice had been smashed or a jade tower had fallen with a crash. Suddenly he returned to his senses. *He felt that he had become Ganto, who throughout all of his life had never come to the slightest harm.* "Wonderful, wonderful," said Hakuin "there is no awakening one must seek."

As Mumon advises in his commentary, one must come face to face with the barbarian, and then one actually knows him. But even in talking about coming face to face we have already obscured the clarity; when is one not face to face with Bodhidharma? To see this requires real training and real satori, and then you can truly become Wakuan.

"Don't discuss your dream/ Before a fool." There is no easy road through this koan. One must drop all reasoning, all search for verbal and intellectual meaning and, naked, stand before Bodhidharma wondering, "Why has that fellow no beard?"

5 Kyogen's Man Up a Tree

*K*yogen explained, *"It is like a man up a tree hanging from a branch by his mouth; his hands can't grasp a bough, his feet won't reach one. Under the tree there is another man, who asks him the meaning of Daruma's coming from the West. If he doesn't answer, he evades his duty. If he answers, he loses his life."*

Mumon's Comment

Even though your eloquence flows like a river, it is of no use whatever. Even though you can explain all the Buddhist sutras, this too is useless. If you can answer the question correctly, you can kill the living, bring the dead back to life. But if you can't answer, you must ask Maitreya when he comes.

Mumon's Verse

> *Kyogen really has bad taste*

Koans: Five

And spreads poison limitlessly.
He stops up the monks' mouths;
Frantically they squeeze tears out from their dead eyes.

Comment

Kyogen was a man of considerable intellectual ability and a great reader. Generally speaking, intellectuals, people who enjoy working with ideas and concepts, have a hard time with Zen practice. To be an intellectual is like being a prisoner with infinitely expandable walls. The freedom thoughts give can be intoxicating. In the realm of thought, if we can imagine it, then it is possible, and if it is possible, then, again in the realm of thought, it is so.

The mind of a human being is something like a Christmas tree with little lights that flash on and off. When a new light turns on a new idea flashes into the mind. On the Christmas tree the lights are all uniform and they remain for a uniform period of time. However, with the mind the lights come in all sizes, and some stay for a long time whereas others stay for a short time.

A star is often to be found at the top of the tree. In the mind this is the central idea—me and the world. It is often called *weltanschauung,* the world idea or the world view. In the ordinary person this light is held in place and supported by all the other lights. Much of the activity of the mind is devoted to maintaining this equilibrium. One of the functions of words is to provide a lattice throughout the mind or consciousness and so give it a constant structure. However, each of the lights can illuminate only its own area. Even the star, although it is the most important of all the lights, can illuminate only the top of the tree.

How are we to illuminate the whole tree? One of the

60

ways most often tried is to build up a picture of the tree
with words and ideas. In this way we can get an idea of
what the tree would look like as a whole. But all that this
does in fact is to put yet another light on the tree, which in
its turn flashes on and off.

Yet some questions demand a whole view of the tree:
what is the meaning of my life? why must I die? what was I
before my parents were born? Isan, Kyogen's teacher, asked
Kyogen such a question. He said, "Forget for the moment
all that you have read and learned. Before you came from
your mothers womb, before you knew this from that, your
real self, tell me, what is it?" What am I? Or, if you like,
Who am I? Isan asks the question in such a way that one is
forced to go beyond the body and all its concerns. He says,
"Before you came from your mother's womb. . . ."
Sometimes the questioner goes back even farther and asks,
"What is your true face, before your parents were born?"
Isan says, "Before you knew this from that. . . ." In other
words, before the discriminating mind, the Christmas tree
mind, has arisen, what is your true self?

What most people will ask themselves is, "From
where, if not the mind, can an answer to such a question
come?" No doubt Kyogen too would have asked himself the
same. The mind, it seems, is the only source of answers. If
the source dries up where is one to go? Isan's question can
be aroused in the mind, but trying to go beyond the mind in
search of a response can only plunge one into the confusion
of darkness. The French philosopher Descartes described
exactly the feeling that Kyogen must have had when, in his
Discourse on Method, he said, "[I am] filled . . . with so
many doubts that it is no longer in my power to forget
them. And yet I do not see in what manner I can resolve

them; and, just as if I had all of a sudden fallen into very deep water, I am so disconcerted that I can neither make certain of setting my feet on the bottom nor can I swim and so support myself on the surface."

It is a basic teaching of Zen, indeed of all Buddhism, that each one is Buddha. The word Buddha has similar roots to *bodhi*, which means the "light of the mind" or "knowing." What is sometimes called enlightenment is coming into one's own light, awakening to one's own knowing. Knowing in this case does not mean knowing this or that, but pure, undefiled, unreflected knowing. When Isan put his question, "your real self, tell me, what is it?" Kyogen knew exactly what he was talking about. Each of us knows, because *each of us is this real self* and the real self is knowing each of us is Buddha. But nevertheless how does one reply? Whatever I say will be understood to be something that is known, not pure knowing. For example, you the reader will no doubt be asking yourself right now, "What does he mean by pure knowing, how can I know it?"

Kyogen in his koan exactly expresses this dilemma: if I say what it is, then that is not it. If he doesn't answer, he evades his duty. If he answers, he will lose his life. It is like a Zen master cautioned, "If you advance one step, you lose sight of the principle. If you retreat one step you fail to keep abreast of things. If you neither advance nor retreat you would be as insensible as stone." A monk asked, "How can we avoid being insensible?" "Advance one step and at the same time retreat one step," replied the master.

Life is always asking us, "What are you?" In earlier days we had ready-made answers: I am a man or woman, I am a soul, I am a spirit, I am the son of God, even I am a farmer or a lord, or a warrior. But in the tormented confusion of the twentieth century we have lost our assurance. Men and women have both lost their assurance in what it means to be the one or the other. With the shifting tides of economics we can no longer cling to the identity we once got from being a manager, a secretary, a miner, a doctor, a lawyer, a mother, a father. With the advance of positivism we now blush when people use such words as soul or spirit. But life is relentless in its demands. "What are you?" Undoubtedly this is a major contributing cause to the epidemic of depression and anxiety that is sweeping our society.

For anyone who is practicing Zen, however, this very confusion is a major asset because life is not interested in any ready-made answers but instead asks, "Beyond all of your identities, what are you?" But be careful, as Kyogen says, it is like a person with no support but his mouth, and if he opens it to reply he crashes to his death; but answer he must. Kyogen was faced, as we all are, with the ultimate dilemma: I know and I must speak, but if I speak I lose what I know and so therefore cannot say it.

6 Buddha Holds Up a Flower

*O*nce long ago when the World-Honored One was at Vulture Peak to give a talk, he simply held a flower up before the assembly. All were silent and did not know what to do, except for venerable Kashyapa who smiled. The World-honored One said, "I have the all-pervading True Dharma Eye, the Marvelous Mind of Nirvana, exquisite teaching of formless form, The Subtle Dharma Gate. It is not dependent on letters and is transmitted outside the scriptures. I now hand it on to Maha Kasho."

Mumon's Comment

Golden-faced Gotama is certainly outrageous. He degrades his noble audience by selling the flesh of dogs while saying it is sheep's head. But one has to admit it is not without genius he does so. However, if everyone that were attending had smiled, to whom would the true dharma have been handed? Or again, if Kasho had not smiled, how would the true dharma have been transmitted? If you say that the open eye of the true dharma can be transmitted, the golden-faced old man with his loud voice deceived the simple villagers. If you say that it cannot be transmitted, then why was Kasho alone approved?

Mumon's Verse

> *Holding up a flower,*
> *The secret is revealed.*
> *Kasho smiles.*
> *Who else knows what to do?*

Comment

We are told that this koan marked the birth of Zen Buddhism. Scholars doubt and debate this fact. Even though it is possible that historically it was not the beginning of Zen, in a very fundamental way it surely was.

Buddha must have been an extremely charismatic man. Wherever he went he collected a great crowd around him. Wandering speakers were an essential element of the time; they took the place of television as they passed on news and information and provided entertainment of a sort. When one of them came into a town it was like number one on the hit parade coming up. So you can just imagine the kind of excitement that Buddha generated. Chances are people would have come from miles around to listen to him talk. You can see the crowd gathering, starting off early in the morning, bringing food, finding themselves a comfortable place, possibly somewhere out of the sun; people with children, women nursing babies. Just imagine the excitement, the hubbub, the general tension that must have developed at the thought of encountering this great teacher whose fame had gone before him.

You can see Buddha, possibly sitting on a high chair provided by a local dignitary, surrounded by his attendants and disciples, and perhaps people bringing him flowers to show their respect. Then everything goes quiet, a hush falls, even the dogs stop barking. Everyone waits for this great man to hold forth.

And he simply holds up a flower.

Can you see it? The people looking at the flower, looking at Buddha, waiting. Then taking a sneaking look at their neighbors, wondering what their reaction is. Then looking back at the flower, asking themselves, what is this about? All except one man, Mahakashyapa. He smiled.

At the Montreal Zen Center we have beginners' courses to help people start Zen practice. The courses are held on four Wednesday evenings, and at the end of each evening I give a small exercise to help people stay mindful during the coming week. The next week at the beginning of the session we discuss what people became aware of while doing the exercise. One of the exercises is introduced by this koan. I tell the koan to the group and say, "If you want to see into this koan you must see into Mahakashyapa's smile. The only way to do this is to *become* Mahakashyapa and so therefore for the coming week I want you to let Mahakashyapa's smile appear on your lips and in your hearts. But, let me caution you, there are different kinds of smiles. I am not asking you to carry a "Pepsodent" smile around. What smile did Mahakashyapa have?"

Naturally, one of the things we discuss is the different kinds of smiles. The one obvious distinction is between sincere and insincere smiles; however, one can also discern other ways of looking at smiles. To help the group get a feel for a particular one I ask them to imagine that they are in the arrivals reception area at an airport. Small groups of people are milling around waiting to greet travelers. One can imagine a man pacing up and down, looking up expectantly every time the door opens, and then frowning, looking down at the ground again and continuing with the pacing. Then, all of a sudden, the door opens and the man looks up. With a broad smile lighting up his face he hurries forward with arms outstretched and embraces the newcomers with hugs and kisses. The embraces are simply an extension of the smile, giving it another dimension. To embrace something is to be one with it. It is like when, at Christmas, one gives a toy to a young child who picks it up and hugs it, beaming with smiles.

This oneness is oneness with what is outside. In another kind of smile the oneness is an inner oneness. For example, you give a written test to a group of children. They sit there frowning at the paper, stealing sidelong glances at one another, sighing, until one of them smiles. You know that child has the answer. It is the smile of comprehension and satisfaction. Until the moment of comprehension, the child was worried, tense, and fidgety. But then it all came together.

The first kind of smile has its aberrant counterpart: the smile of the used car salesman. Hamlet remarks, "A man can smile, smile, smile and still be a damned villain!" We have learned to use the smile, to make it work for us. We have commercialized it. The second kind of smile also has its ugly sister. It is the smile of superiority, the sardonic smile, that cuts one off from others, the smile that makes one an island.

Now we must ask ourselves whether Mahakashyapa's smile was the first or second. Was it a smile by which he embraced all those present, a smile of communication, a coming together with the outside world? Or was it a smile of understanding, "I've got it!" It might seem that by looking inside and outside we have covered all bases. If it is not the one, it must be the other. But a third kind of smile is possible: Mahakashyapa's smile. What kind of smile could this be?

On one occasion I was traveling home on the Montreal subway. The car was fairly full, and it was at that time in the afternoon when everyone seems weary; a dull, heavy, unreal atmosphere had descended on us all. Each traveler was in intimate contact with others, but steadfastly avoiding eye contact, and therefore avoiding all acknowledgment of the presence of others.

In the car was a little black child, about two years old. He was sitting upright in his stroller, back straight, head up. All of a sudden he looked around the car out of his big wide eyes and smiled. Then the unexpected, one might almost say the impossible, happened. We all smiled. Not only did we smile with the baby, but, and this is on the Montreal subway, we smiled at one another! The smile rippled around the car like a butterfly. People made eye contact with each other and smiled. What was also surprising was that, when the train stopped at the next station, people also smiled as they entered the car, although they could hardly have had any idea of what it was that they were smiling at or for. One could say that when the baby smiled, the whole world smiled. Similarly, one could say that when Mahakashyapa smiled, not only did the flower smile, but the world was one smiling flower.

It is through the smile that the light of love, the One, shines through. We speak of one whose face shines with happiness, whose face is lit up by a smile, we say he was beaming when we mean he was smiling. Exodus tells us when Moses came down from his encounter with the One on the Mount of Sinai, "all the children of Israel saw the face of Moses, that the skin of Moses' face shone. . . ." Within all smiles is this light; however, the light of unity within the smile we direct to others and the light of unity within the smile of comprehension, is reflected by the situation in which it occurs. With Mahakashyapa the light was not reflected, it emanated straight from the source. Like the baby, he just smiled. If we can smile with Mahakashyapa, we smile as Mahakashyapa, we do not smile at or because of anything. It is nonobstruction that is transmitted from heart to heart. The marvelous mind of Nirvana, the exquisite teaching of formless form, the subtle dharma gate are all in the smile.

But what kind of smile is this? This same smile is echoed in the irony of Mumon when he calls Buddha a huckster selling "Dog's flesh advertised as sheep's head." Instead of giving the people a tasty dish of eloquence, he served up just one flower. But then what food can one give to those who are filled to overflowing?

But before leaving this koan let us ask again what it was exactly that was transmitted. A governor asked Master Ungo, "It is said, the World-Honored One gave a secret talk of holding up a flower and Kasho by smiling did not conceal it. What does this mean?" Ungo called out, "O, Governor!" "Yes, Master," replied the governor. "Do you understand?" asked Ungo. When the governor replied, "No, I don't," Ungo told him, "If you do not understand, it shows that the

World-Honored One did make the secret talk. If you do understand, it means that Kasho did not conceal it."

Dogen said, "Every country has the true flower: beautiful, undefiled truth. Even though this truth abounds with peace and tranquillity, the ordinary person cannot understand it." He also said, "The true flower shows the truth simultaneously with the truth showing the true flower."

7 Joshu Says, "Wash Your Bowl"

A monk once said to Joshu, "I have just come to the monastery. Will you please teach me?" Joshu asked, "Have you had your breakfast?" "Yes," said the monk. "Then wash your bowl," Joshu told him.

Mumon's Comment
Joshu opened his mouth and showed his gallbladder, and revealed his heart and liver. If this monk, hearing it, failed to grasp it, he would mistake a bell for a pot.

Mumon's Verse

> *Because it is so clear*
> *It takes a longer time to realize it.*
> *If you immediately know candle light is fire,*
> *Then the meal was cooked a long time ago.*

Comment

It is probably best to see this koan as a dharma duel. In this case the monk who asks Joshu for his teaching would not be a novice, but would be well advanced. Buried in his question would be a barb, because is there a teaching of Zen? In the *Diamond Sutra* Buddha asks Subhuti, "Have I a doctrine to teach?" And Subhuti says, "No!" How would you respond if someone were to ask you, "What is the teaching of Zen?" If it is someone who knows nothing, or very little, you might talk about zazen posture, or the need to wake up, or the importance of being mindful during the day. But what if the questioner was well versed in all that, and had practiced Zen for a long while. How would you then respond?

A similar *mondo* (question and answer) took place between Joshu and another monk who admitted, "I have just come to the monastery. I know nothing about Zen." In other words, "Teach me Zen." Joshu asked, "What is your name?" "Enan," replied the monk. "That is some 'know nothing,'" retorted Joshu.

Is Joshu teaching the monk? One might say that he is explaining that at his monastery he has a guideline that says people must always wash their bowls after meals. Or it might be that he is teaching housekeeping, that one should be neat and orderly; orderliness is a sign of spiritual maturity.

I remember once, when I returned to the dressing room of a swimming pool after having swum. One other person was there and he was just finishing dressing. After he finished he bent down and wiped up the water that was on the floor where he had dried himself. My first thought was, "He must have been a monk!" When he stood up and was about to leave, I caught his eye and we started a conversation. It turned out that he was indeed a former monk, and when I commented on his cleaning the floor he looked quite surprised. It was obviously something that to him was second nature. I could not help thinking about the nun who, when asked why the community cleaned the convent thoroughly each day, responded, "Why not, do you not wash your face each day?"

What is the teaching of Zen? Have you dried yourself? Then wipe up the floor.

Another interpretation that is sometimes given is that when Joshu asked if the monk had had his meal he really meant, "Have you come to awakening?" When the monk says yes, Joshu advises, "Then go ahead and clean up the defilements that are still in the mind." But if the koan is indicating something that could be put just as well in straightforward language, what is the value of someone devoting time and energy to penetrate it? Why not just say it? We must remember that, as Yasutani Roshi pointed out, any koan can be used as a breakthrough koan. "Is the rice cooked yet?" was what the fifth patriarch asked Hui Neng, but it was a concrete way of asking about Hui Neng's inner state. Even so, it was not a koan that the patriarch was giving Hui Neng.

Neither of the above interpretations qualifies as a response to a koan. Neither has the kind of bite we have come to realize is the hallmark of a koan. It is true that if one is living in a community, some rules relating to orderliness and neatness are imperative for the general good. It is also true that most monasteries have strict housekeeping rules. Furthermore, after the first awakening, the student does have a long and difficult time ahead in which all the defilements of long years must be cleansed. But to teach these kinds of things does not require a koan.

Mumon in his commentary says, "Joshu opened his mouth and showed his gallbladder, and revealed his heart and liver." Everything was revealed in "Wash your bowl." What does it mean to say that? There is nothing hidden about Joshu's Zen, nothing that has to be teased out, understood, learned, and remembered. For Joshu to live a Zen life was not to live a *Zen-like* life; living life just as it is, is Zen.

Let me repeat, to get to the heart of this koan, for the time being we must assume the monk who seems to be asking Joshu such an innocuous question is deeply awakened. He is asking, "What is Joshu's teaching, what is Joshu's Zen?" Buried in his question is a double bind, a situation in which one is damned if one does and damned if one doesn't.

As we know, neither a koan nor a Zen master teaches anything. In the *Hekiganroku* master Hyakujo berates his monks for traveling around listening to different Zen teachers. He calls them "mash eaters," those who devour what is left over after the essence has been extracted. "Don't you know," he demanded, "that in the whole of China there are no teachers of Zen?" What is it you need to know? There is no "way" to awakening other than by awakening itself.

However, suppose that Joshu had said, "Me, I don't have any teaching!" No doubt the monk would have turned on his heel and walked away, possibly saying over his shoulder, "Then what are you doing as head of a monastery?" To say koans have no teaching, invites the question, "Then why did you spend twenty years working on them?"

What is your teaching? With this question we go to the very heart of the difficulty of Zen practice. To say it is this or that or something else simply leads the beginner astray and leaves the one who knows, laughing. Knowledge is an addition, something extra. It is said in Zen that what comes through the front door is not the treasure of the house. A master said, "Do not let the word Tao delude you. Realize it is nothing else than what you do morning and night." So Joshu replies, "Have you had your breakfast? Then wash your bowl."

Instead of asking "What is your teaching," the monk could equally well have asked, "What is the most profound thing that you can say?" or "What is it that, by knowing it, everything in the universe is known?" How then is Joshu's answer the most profound thing that he could say? Someone might say Joshu is implying that when washing the bowl the monk should be completely present. This indeed is the case, and an answer such as that might well be a lot more worth while than the other possible replies that were suggested. But what about the word "should"? We say *should* when we understand the truth but cannot live it. Indeed, in Joshu's response is the very elimination of the *should*, the elimination of the gap between understanding and action. That is the profundity of Joshu's reply, which calls on us not simply to know the truth, but to live it.

Joshu was not prepared for the question. Perhaps he was helping in the garden, or maybe just walking at ease in the early morning sun. The monk sees the great man and recognizes him immediately. "Let's see if we can trip him up," is perhaps the motivating thought, and so out of the blue comes his question; and without pause Joshu replies. Mumon said, "If you know at once that candle light is fire, then the meal has long been cooked." The rice has been long cooked: from the beginning all beings are Buddha.

8 Keichu's Wheel

Zen master Gettan said to a monk, "Keichu made a hundred carts. If we took off the wheels and removed the axle, what would be left?"

Mumon's Comment

To clarify this, one's eye should be like a shooting star, one's response a flash of lightning.

Mumon's Verse

When the wheel of mind-activity whirs
Even a master doesn't know how to cope.
It moves in all directions in heaven and earth,
North, south, east, and west.

Comment

Keichu was a master wheelwright, and so the carts he made

would have been perfect. But that is not of relevance. It could be any old cart, and the koan asks, if you take it to pieces and throw away the pieces, what would be left? On the face of it the answer is so obvious: nothing! But that will not do. As innocuous as it may seem, this koan goes right to the heart of human terror. When one takes away your arms, legs, and head, what will be left? Again many people dread the answer, which, they feel, is also so obvious—*nothing*.

We look around us and see a world. Things are there in space, in time. They come and they go, and when they are gone we believe they leave behind nothing. Other people come and go. They, too, leave behind, nothing. But when have you ever encountered nothing? Someone asks, "What is in that drawer?" So you look and see it is empty. "Nothing," you say. "There is nothing in the drawer." But have you encountered nothing? The absence, the nothing is not in the drawer. It is in your own mind.

Not only this, but are things out there in space and time? Have you ever really looked or have you just taken it for granted? Of course the problem is that when one does really look one does so in a completely artificial way, a way that implies things are indeed out there. But when you are driving along the highway amid dozens of cars, some cutting in, some slowing down, some speeding up, some merging from off the ramp, do you see cars? Highway signs flash by, overpasses, underpasses; are they not all part of one intricate, ever-changing pattern? One responds to *patterns* and events, not things, not cars. If one does become fixated on a particular thing, a car or a sign, one can get vertigo, one feels less in control, unsteady. Because the patterns change constantly the metaphor of the kaleidoscope inevitably comes to mind. If one could only see without looking one would know the world to be like a dream in which there is not me and you, me and the world, but one seamless whole. As Huang Po says, "There is only One Mind and not a particle of anything else on which to lay hold."

Another way of asking the koan's question is in the *Surangama Sutra,* in which it is asked, "When the bell stops ringing, does the ear stop hearing?" When there is nothing to hear, do you stop hearing or do you hear nothing? Again, a ready-made response leaps to mind, "When the bell stops ringing I don't hear anything at all." But what is this not hearing? Silence? But then do we not *hear* silence? Beyond silence and sound, what then?

> *When the wheel of mind-activity whirs*
> *Even a master doesn't know how to cope.*
> *It moves in all directions in heaven and earth,*
> *North, south, east, and west.*

The mind's activity is churning out thoughts, dreams, expectations, prejudices, and beliefs without end. When the mind moves, myriad worlds appear. All of history, the arts and sciences, literature, philosophies, theologies, all the laws and rules of all the innumerable societies past, present, and future, all come out of one mind that is unmoved by it all. Again to quote Huang Po, "Mind is like vast space in which there is no confusion or evil, as when the sun wheels through it shining upon the four corners of the world. For, when the sun rises and illuminates the whole earth, space gains not in brilliance; and, when the sun sets space does not darken. The phenomena of light and dark alternate with each other, but the nature of the void remains unchanged. So it is with the mind of the Buddha and of sentient beings."

"The phenomena of light and darkness alternate with

each other," but the nature of the void remains unchanged. Carts appear and disappear, parts are added and taken away, but the nature of the void remains unchanged. What is this void? It is not nothing. To see into that, Mumon says, "One's eye should be like a shooting star, one's response a flash of lightning" unmediated by thought, unobstructed by what you believe.

9 Daitsu Chisho Buddha

A monk asked Koyo Seijo, "Daitsu Chisho Buddha sat in zazen for eons and eons and could not attain Buddhahood. Why was this?" Seijo said, "That's a good question." The monk persisted, "He meditated so long; why did he not become Buddha?" Seijo warned, "Don't overdo it."

Mumon's Comment

I can accept the barbarian's realization, what I can't accept is his understanding. When an ordinary person gets it, he is a sage. When a sage understands it, he is just an ordinary person.

Mumon's Verse

> It is better to liberate your mind than your body;
> When the mind is liberated, the body is liberated.

Daitsu Chisho Buddha

When both body and mind are liberated
What more is there to get?

Comment

Rinzai called Daitsu Chisho Buddha "The Buddha of Supreme Penetration and Surpassing Wisdom," and said: "'Supreme Penetration' means one personally sees into the complete absence of form and self nature in the ten thousand dharmas. 'Surpassing Wisdom' means to be without doubt of any kind and to be clear without even a speck of dust. 'Buddha' means purity of mind whose radiance pervades the ten directions. 'To sit for ten kalpas' means to practice the ten paramitas. 'The Buddhadharma did not manifest' means Buddha is in essence birthless and dharmas in essence without end. Why then should it manifest? 'He did not attain Buddhahood' means Buddha cannot become Buddha."

When one encounters this koan for the first time one has a picture of Daitsu Chisho Buddha struggling year after futile year trying to become Buddha. And one is tempted to give a quick answer: Buddha cannot become Buddha. But when the monk asks why Chisho Buddha could not attain Buddhahood after eons of zazen, Koyo Seijo nods, "That is a good question." One could say the koan revolves around this remark of the master. Why does the master say the question is a good one if the answer is simply that it is a waste of time for Buddha to try to become Buddha? It is evident the master is quite serious, because when the monk starts trying to capitalize on his question, the master shuts him up. Why is the monk's question a good one? What is it really asking?

How can Buddha become Buddha implies Daitsu Chisho Buddha should give up all his efforts and just realize he is Buddha. In Zen Buddhism two schools emerged and are still extant: Rinzai and Soto. The struggle to realize his Buddhahood could be looked on as the way of the Rinzai sect. To give up all efforts and realize one is Buddha is the way of the Soto sect. Both are only half the answer, but how do you add them together to make them into a whole way? That is what the koan is about.

The koan is also about Daitsu Chisho Buddha and what it means to be awakened. One quite common belief is that awakening is the end of all activity, the end of all problems and tribulations. People sometimes ask in all seriousness, "What does one do after coming to awakening?" However, when we have seen into koan 2, Hyakujo's Fox, we realize this is a very naive belief. When commenting on that koan we quoted a Mahayana text: "Just so the Bodhisattva, when he comprehends the dharmas as he should, does not retire into blessed rest. In wisdom then he dwells." We pointed out blessed rest, or nivriti, is the Nirvana that excludes the world of suffering.

What is the nature of Daitsu Chisho Buddha? In *The Butterfly's Dream* I recounted the story of ten people who had to cross a river that was quite swollen after a heavy storm. Once the group had got across, one of them suggested they should count the members to ensure all had succeeded in making it. He stepped forward and counted 1 2 3 4 5 6 7 8 9. He turned in alarm and said, "We have lost one of the group." Another counted and came to the same number. The group was bewailing the loss of a member when a stranger walked by. After hearing of the problem the stranger said he would count and proceeded to do so: 1 2 3 4 5 6 7 8 9 10. But he too was mistaken and, if you think he should have counted 11, you too are mistaken.

How do you count the one who cannot be counted? How do you count the one who counts?

We understand logically what is involved in the above story, but can we realize what is involved? It is the same with Daitsu Chisho Buddha. We understand Buddha cannot become Buddha, but do we realize what this means? This is why the master said the question is a good one.

Perhaps the following dialogue taken from the *Vilmalakirti Sutra,* a Mahayana sutra held in very high esteem by Zen Buddhists, will help. In one section of this sutra Sariputra, a senior disciple of Buddha, asks a goddess how long it will be before she attains full awakening. The goddess says: "It is impossible that I should attain full awakening of Buddhahood!" She then explains that full awakening is not something to be attained. Because it is impossible to do so, no one attains the perfect awakening of Buddhahood. Sariputra objects and says the Buddhas of the past, present, and future have all attained perfect awakening, but the goddess chides him, "'The Buddhas of the past, present, and future' is a conventional phrase made up of a certain number of syllables. The Buddhas are neither present, past, nor future. Their awakening transcends the three times." Then she asks Sariputra, "Have you attained awakening?" Sariputra says it is attained because there is no attainment. The goddess replies, "Just so, there is perfect awakening because there is no attainment of perfect awakening."

The logic is impeccable, but let us remember Mumon's comment, "I can accept the barbarian's realization, what I can't accept is his understanding. When an ordinary person gets it, he is a sage. When a sage understands it, he is just an ordinary person." What is the difference between realization and understanding?

10 Poor Seizei

*S*eizei complained to Sozan, "Seizei is quite destitute. Will you give him food?" Sozan called out "Seizei!" Seizei responded, "Yes, Sir!" Sozan scolded, "You have finished three cups of the finest wine in China and still you say you have not yet moistened your lips!"

Mumon's Comment

Seizei pretended to retreat. What was his scheme? Sozan had the eye of Buddha and saw through his opponent's motive. However, I want to ask you, at what point did Seizei drink wine?

Mumon's Verse

> Poverty like Hanzen's,
> Mind like Kou's;

With no means of livelihood,
He dares to rival the richest.

Comment

All koans are an invitation to awaken to our true mind, therefore only one response is ever available and this response is awakening. This makes koans difficult because the awakened state is completely free, empty of all restraints and restrictions, uncluttered even by a speck of dust, as one Zen master put it. In contrast, the unawakened mind treasures experiences, memories, opinions, and prejudices. These together, people think of as their mind, their life. They search therefore for a rich life, a cultivated mind, a life full of diverse experiences, pleasant memories, abundant and available knowledge, many friends, and lots of possessions. But as we grow older it often happens the richness goes out of life, and some people then seek thrills, the extraordinary, the exotic, the bizarre, the dangerous, or the forbidden, hoping these will somehow shock the mind awake once more. Others reflect on what might have been, yearn for what is not, and grow bitter.

But sometimes, "distracted from distraction by distraction," we wonder how we can restore the lost magic of childhood: perhaps some summer's day we heard the song of a bird with unimpeded clarity; or at some moment we saw the world of trees, grass, wildflowers and streams as though for the first time. We long for such innocence to return.

Each year people go on holiday and return refreshed and rejuvenated. What was it about the holiday that brought them back to life? Was it the sun, the sand, the smell of the sea? Yes, it was all of these. Was it the fact that they were away from the telephone, away from people calling on them, away from the problems these would bring? Yes, it was this too. But beyond all of that, what was it that rejuvenated them? What was it that gave the sea, the sun, and the sand their power?

On holiday walking along the beach, having made an agreement with ourselves to pretend for the time being problems do not exist, we *feel* the sand, we *feel* the shock of the water as we wade, we *smell* the salt and the sea. We *see* the seagull swooping down. We *hear* the steady pounding of the surf against the rocks, we *taste* the food. In short, *we are present*. Many people eat while reading the newspaper or looking at television, they walk along worrying about some argument they have had or about some problem they have at work. They hear other people speaking but only through a curtain of criticism and envy. They are not present, and so life has lost its magic.

This koan is about the magic of the mind, the magic of being present, the magic that makes of every day a good day.

The poverty of Seizei is not ordinary poverty, but that of the poor in spirit who, Jesus said, are blessed "for they shall see God." Therefore Seizei was no ordinary monk but, on the contrary, one who was deeply awakened.

A Tibetan story tells of a man who went to a master to ask for his teaching. The master said, "First you must bring me all that you possess." The man went back home, gathered together all his worldly possessions, and set off back to the master. After he had gone a short distance the man remembered an old lame goat that he had left behind. "The master will surely not want that goat," he thought. When he arrived the master asked him, "Is this everything that you own." The man said, "Yes, except for an old lame goat that I felt sure you would not want," "Go and get the goat," said the master.

T.S. Eliot described the spiritual state as:

A condition of utter simplicity
Costing not less than everything[3]

A Zen master snatches even the dried crust from the hands of a starving man because, as master Ummon warns, "Even a good thing is not as good as no thing."

A conversation between the contemporary Hindu master Nisargadatta and a visitor helps us to understand what is implied by this poverty. The visitor asked Nisargadatta about the yogin helping others, and Nisargadatta says, "There are no others to help. A rich man when he hands over his entire fortune to his family has not a coin to give a beggar." So is the wise man stripped of all his powers and possessions. Nothing, literally nothing can be said about him. He cannot help anyone for he is everyone. He is the poor and also his poverty, the thief and his thievery. How can he be said to help when he is not apart. Who thinks of himself as separate from the world, let him help the world.

Mumon, in his poem, likens the poverty of Seizei to that of Hanzen. Hanzen was a famous Chinese scholar who was appointed to the high post of governor. He did not accept the post, however, but instead took care of his ailing mother. His contentment with honest poverty and his filial devotion made his name renowned. This is the poverty of Hanan that is not only accepted but chosen, not only chosen but forgotten.

Kou, to whom Mumon also refers, was a legendary hero in Chinese history. He commanded an army in battle

---

[3] *The Four Quartets.* T. S. Eliot. (London: Faber and Faber, 1944).

against an enemy and won all the battles except his last. Even though he was surrounded by the army of the enemy, he spent the evening at ease with his mistress Gu, whom he loved dearly, unflinching in the face of death. He sang a song that became famous:

> *Even with strength to move mountains,*
> *And spirit enough for the whole world,*
> *All is lost;*
> *Sui my horse not yet dead.*
> *Gu! Oh Gu! What is your fate?*

Kou's mind was steadfast and secure. It is in such a steadfast and secure mind that Seizei is able to be at home in his poverty.

Our first question is "What is Sozan's poverty?" and to know this we must enter into it, we must be poor Seizei. Then we must understand Sozan's calling him and telling him that he has drunk of the finest wine in China. What is this wine? A monk, when he became awakened wrote:

> *In a moonlight night on a spring day*
> *The croak of a frog*
> *Pierces through the whole cosmos and turns it into a*
> *   single family.*
> *To see into this is to see truly that every day is a good*
> *   day.*

11 Joshu's Hermits

*J*oshu went to a hermit's hut and called, "Is anyone at home? Is anyone at home?" The hermit thrust up his fist. Joshu said, "The water is too shallow to anchor here," and went away. He went to another hermit's hut and cried out, "Is anyone at home? Is anyone at home?" The hermit thrust up a fist. Joshu said, "Freely you give, freely you take away. Freely you bestow life, freely you destroy," and made a profound bow.

Mumon's Comment

Both stuck up their fist; why was one accepted, the other rejected? Just say, where is the source of the confusion between the two? If, in regard to this you can speak a word of understanding, then you will realize that Joshu's tongue has no bone in it. Now he raises up, now he dashes down, in perfect freedom. But though this is so, remember that the two hermits also saw through Joshu. Furthermore, if you say one or other of the two hermits is better or worse, you do not have an open eye. Neither do you have an open eye if you suppose there is no difference between the two hermits.

Mumon's Verse

> *His eye a shooting star,*
> *He moves like lightning.*
> *A death dealer,*
> *A life-giving sword.*

Comment

It will be as well to give a little background to this koan. Joshu was famous for, among other things, quoting *Verses on the Faith Mind* by the third patriarch. This is a fairly long poem written to exhort the follower of the Way to go beyond judgments of good and bad. For example, the verses begin with the lines:

> *The Great Way is not difficult*
> *For those who have no preferences.*
> *When one no longer chooses*
> *The way stands clear and wide open*
>
> *But if you make the slightest distinction*
> *Heaven and earth are split far apart.* [4]

In the *Hekiganroku* are several koans in which monks challenge Joshu for his adherence to the verses of the faith mind. One monk said, "You often quote, 'The Great Way is not difficult/ For those who have no preferences,' but aren't you thereby having a preference?"

This exhortation, which is basic to Zen teaching, to go beyond good and bad is often misunderstood. For example, some might feel that one should not make judgments of any

---

[4] Chant version prepared by the Rochester Zen Center.

kind. On one occasion I was drawn into a conversation about a Zen teacher who was given a very expensive car as a present. The conversation devolved on whether or not the teacher should have accepted the present, and I was asked to give my opinion. I said that I felt that, because of the circumstances surrounding the gift, he should not have accepted it and that he had made a mistake in doing so. Later one of the members of the center confessed to me he had been very upset with my response and had asked himself what worth I had as a teacher if I would make such judgments while at the same time urging people to go beyond good and bad.

However, it is impossible to live life without making judgments. All the time one asks oneself whether it would be better to do one thing rather than another. This teacher had the choice of accepting or not accepting the car; at the time the question was put to me I had to judge whether it were better to answer than not to answer. The problem is, however, that we tend to raise our judgments to the status of the absolute. There is a difference between judging a person to be mistaken and judging them to be morally wrong. Morally wrong implies an absolute, and it is this absolute that is in question. It implies that good and bad exist independently of each other.

Others, misunderstanding the injunction to go beyond good and bad, believe they can ignore the rules of common decency. We already explored this attitude in Hyakujo's Fox and will not repeat it.

This koan then is about what it means to go beyond good and bad. Indeed, to go further, it is also a koan that is about what it means to get beyond all contraries. However, let it be repeated that what is at issue is getting *beyond* the opposites, not abandoning them. Furthermore, *beyond* does not mean some higher, more exalted realm. When we look at a vase we can admire the beauty, wonder at the cost, imagine the use it can be put to, and scheme about how we can make it our own. We can also go beyond the form of the vase and be interested instead in the clay of which it was made; the considerations of beauty, use, cost, and ownership drop away and a new set of considerations now comes into focus.

In this regard there is a mondo in which someone asked Joshu, "The one who is beyond good and bad, is he liberated or not?" Joshu answered, "He is not." The questioner continued, "Why not?" Joshu retorted, "Because he is within good and evil!" Is this not what the koan is pointing out?

A koan in the *Hekiganroku* is the reciprocal of the one we are dealing with. A monk named Mayoku comes to master Shokei carrying his staff with him. He walks around the master three times, shakes his staff and sticks it into the ground, and stands up straight. Shokei says, "Right!" Mayoku then goes to Zen master Nansen, walks around him three times, shakes his staff, sticks it into the ground and stands up straight. Nansen says, "Wrong!" Mayoku then asks, "Shokei said 'Right,' why do you say 'Wrong?'" Nansen says, "Shokei is right but you are wrong. You are blown about by the wind. That will lead to destruction."

One is tempted to think that the two masters are in some way testing the monk to see his reaction. Will he be upset by this kind of rough handling? If so, is his practice mature? Two objections must be made about this interpretation. The first is that one does not need a koan to bring such a point home. If, as we say, all koans have a bite, then where in the koan would the bite be if such an interpretation is accepted? The second objection to an interpretation such as this is that it is not valid in any case. People react to situations not so much according to their spiritual maturity as according to their temperament. People who are naturally phlegmatic are difficult to arouse, but those who are made of fire respond swiftly and sometimes dramatically. Furthermore, it is a mistake to believe Zen training produces people who never react with heat. Harada Roshi was a fiery, dynamic man and, Roshi Kapleau told us, still could become angry many years after his awakening. Harada Roshi used to say that the anger of an awakened person is like snowflakes falling on a hot stove. We must remember that Jesus went into a rage at the merchants who were desecrating the temple by selling their goods there, and Hakuin's writing often displays more spleen than some people like to see in a Zen master.

Once we can see the koan from the *Hekiganroku* as the reciprocal of Joshu's two hermits and also see them both within the context of the third patriarch's *Verses on the Faith Mind*, it becomes evident that they are about what it means to go beyond good and bad. In Joshu's koan he is the judge, and the two hermits the judged. The koan from the *Hekiganroku* has two judges, Shokei and Nansen, and one judged: Mayoku. Let us put them together and we get: Joshu goes to see a hermit and calls out "Is anyone there?" The hermit raises his fist and Joshu says, "Good," then two minutes later says "Bad." No, let us leave out the two minutes; he says, "Good-bad."

Returning to the koan as given, its bite comes from the question: if "the Great Way is not difficult for those who have no preferences," what is Joshu doing displaying preferences? Moreover, why does he say good in the first case and bad in the second, even though it is one situation, thrusting up a fist, that is being judged?

One of the problems that taxed the brains of medieval theologians was the question, "If God is good and all-powerful, where does evil in the world come from?" Or if, as the Hebrew religion insists, "The Lord our God, the Lord is One," where did the devil come from? As I pointed out in *The Iron Cow of Zen*, one is faced with either an ontological unity, God is one and therefore an ethical duality, God is good and bad; or an ethical unity, God is good, and therefore an ontological duality of two Gods, a good one and a bad one. Put as baldly as possible the problem is how can one be two? How can one be good-bad?

We have to see the quandary at the back of the koan. Joshu calls out, "Is anyone there?" The hermit thrusts up a hand. This is the first barrier. Pass it and the rest of the koan will fall into place. What is there in the raising of the hand? It is certainly not as at school when a teacher called our name and we raised our hand saying, in effect, "I am here." It was not raised in salute either. One has to do it to know it. In other words one has to know the thrust up fist from within, not from outside.

Huang Po wrote, "The phenomena of light and darkness alternate with each other, but the nature of the void remains unchanged. So it is with the mind of the Buddha and of sentient beings." One must be careful that one does not make the void a separate state of being.

Another master said, "Heaven and earth the whole world is just oneself, when cold it is cold throughout heaven and earth; when hot, it is hot throughout heaven and earth. When it exists, all throughout heaven and earth exist; when it doesn't exist, heaven and earth do not exist. When affirmed all throughout heaven and earth is; when denied all throughout heaven and earth is not."

Yet another observed, "The bitter melon is bitter through and through; the sweet melon is sweet through and through."

When Mumon says, "He is a death dealer, a life-giving sword," he is referring to Joshu, who, as Mumon also reveals, the monks saw into.

12 Zuigan Calls, "Master"

*E*very day Master Zuigan would call out to himself,
   "Oh, Master!" and would answer himself, "Yes?"
"Wake up, wake up!" he would cry, and would answer
"Yes, yes!" "Don't be deceived by others, at any time, day
or night." "No, I will not."

Mumon's Comment

Old Zuigan sells himself and buys himself. He has lots of
masks of goblins and devils to play with. How so? Look and
see! A calling mask, an answering mask, an awake mask,
and one that will not be deceived by others. If you take
these different appearances as really existing, you are altogether mistaken. Simply to imitate Zuigan would be simply
to have the understanding of a fox.

Mumon's Verse

Those who search for a way do not know the true
nature of the self;
They only know their old discriminating mind.
This mind is the cause of the endless cycle of birth and
  death,
Yet ignorant people take it for the original man.

Comment

Who is the master? Is it the one who called out "Oh, Master!" or the one who called out "Yes?" Furthermore, when Zuigan warns, "Do not be deceived by others," does he mean do not be deceived by what others say or do? Or does he mean something else?

Jean Paul Sartre, in his play *No Exit*, wrote, "Hell is other people." He was, in Zuigan's terms, deceived by others. According to Christianity, we are all children of a common God, a common father. According to Buddhism, we are closer than this, closer than kin. John Donne, a seventeenth-century British poet, said, ". . . Never send to know for whom the bell tolls, it tolls for thee." One could say he was not deceived by others.

A remarkable phenomenon that has come to our notice in recent years is multiple personalities: one body inhabited by a number, sometimes a great number, of personalities each calling itself "I." In men are found female personalities, in women, male personalities. Often these personalities do not know of the existence of the others. Each has its own special set of memories, its own likes and dislikes, its own way of walking and talking. Some even prefer another language to the one spoken by others in the same body.

One of the ways to cure the person so afflicted is to merge the personalities into one whole. For the individual personalities, however, to be merged is tantamount to dying, and some of the personalities are as afraid of merging as people are of dying. One case is on record in which the personality to be merged insisted that a priest be consulted to ensure that her soul would not suffer as a consequence. Naturally, many people, including many psychologists, resist the idea of multiple personalities because it throws into question the whole idea of the integrity of the individual. Is it possible, however, that we are all a personality of a multiple personality? Is Buddha a multiple personality? The master that Zuigan calls to, is he a multiple personality?

We are so secure in our knowledge of I, the one who is in control, or at least we like to think of it as so. But is this I really the one in control? What happens when I goes to sleep, or faints? One can ask, who is it who speaks, who is it who sees and hears? We say "I" do, but who is the master?

Jewish philosopher Martin Buber suggested that I on its own is an abstraction; the concrete fact is *I-Thou* or *I-It*. In other words I is but one element in a complex situation. But are there two I's; the I of I-It and the I of I-Thou? Perhaps our security in what we call I is misplaced and, because of this misplaced security, we might be missing something very important. This something important furthermore does not simply have a philosophical value, but a value that makes the difference between life and death. For example, given that all of these I's, or masks of goblins and demons, exist, which, if any, will survive death?

A Zen master came to awakening on seeing himself reflected in the water. He wrote a verse that included the following lines:

I meet him wherever I go.
He is the same as me,
Yet I am not he!
Only if you understand this
Will you accord with what you are.

This is similar to what a Sufi teacher said about Allah. Allah is reputed to have said, "I was a hidden treasure and yearned to be known. Then I created creatures in order to be known by them." It looks as though Zuigan is doing the same. Mumon identified ". . . lots of masks of goblins and devils. . . . A calling mask, an answering mask, an awake mask, and one that will not be deceived by others." The Latin for "mask" is *persona,* from which we derive "personality." If I had no personality what would I be? But am I simply a personality? Again Mumon vows, "If you take these different appearances as really existing, you are altogether mistaken."

13 Tokusan Carries His Bowls

One day Tokusan went to the dining room carrying his bowls. Seppo, the head cook, asked, "What are you doing here with your bowls? The bell has not rung, nor has the drum been struck." Tokusan turned and went back to his room. Seppo told Ganto about this, and Ganto concluded, "Tokusan is well known as a great teacher, but even so he doesn't know the last word of Zen." Tokusan heard about this remark and sent his attendant to fetch Ganto. "Do you not approve of my teaching?" he asked. Ganto whispered to Tokusan. Tokusan was silent.

The next day Tokusan ascended the rostrum as usual, but this time his teisho was quite different. Ganto, going to the front of the hall, clapped his hands and laughed loudly, saying, "Congratulations! The old man has got the last word! From now on, nobody will be able to take the rise out of him!"

Mumon's Comment

As for the last word, it has never entered the mind of Ganto nor of Tokusan! When you come to look at it, you find they are both like puppets on the shelf.

Mumon's Verse

> *To know the first word*
> *Is to know the last;*
> *But neither the first nor the last*
> *Is a word.*

Comment

To be able to work with this koan one must have some understanding of the people involved. Tokusan, before he became a Zen Buddhist, used to expound the *Diamond Sutra* (excerpts of which are given in Appendix 1, and you might care to read them before going on with this commentary). An account of his awakening is given in koan 28. It is sufficient at this time simply to say he was a deeply awakened man, and during his life was a fiery teacher fond of using the stick to cajole his monks to greater efforts. At the time of this koan he was an old man and fully mature.

One could say that Seppo and Ganto stood in the relation of younger and older brothers. At the time of the koan Seppo was highly developed, but he still had not dropped the bottom out of the bucket. A little knowledge is dangerous, and sometimes a little wisdom is no less dangerous. Ganto was older and wiser, and, as the following story of Seppo's full awakening shows, on occasions he took the place of Seppo's teacher.

After Tokusan's death, while Seppo and Ganto were on a journey, they were caught in a severe snow storm and had to find shelter for several days at an inn. Ganto spent the time relaxing and sleeping, while Seppo struggled through the days and nights in zazen. One day, Seppo became so furious he shouted at Ganto, "Get up! Get out of bed!" Ganto groaned, "But why should I?" Seppo retorted, "Why is it that I have to be burdened with a load like this? He's just one big drag! All he ever does or wants to do is sleep." Ganto shouted back, "Do be quiet and go to sleep! Not a day goes by but you are sitting up there like some Buddha figure!" Seppo pointed to his heart and said, "Here I have no peace. I can't pretend otherwise." Ganto expressed surprise at this and asked Seppo to tell him about his practice. After Seppo had done so, Ganto exclaimed, "Haven't you heard that what enters by the door is not the treasure of the house? It is what comes from the very depths of your heart that moves heaven and earth." It was at this Seppo came to deep awakening.

"What comes in by the front door is not the treasure of the house." This in its way is a key to the koan. The koan can be looked on as a drama having three acts, each of which contains a number of pressing questions. Central to the koan is what Ganto whispers to Tokusan after the latter asks, "Do you do not approve of my teaching?"; if one can enter into that, the whole koan falls into place. But to do this one must know what is in Tokusan's mind as he goes back to the room. And to see the full significance of the koan one has to know what it was about Tokusan's talk the next day that made it so different.

Tokusan's awakening occurred when he was relatively young, and for a long time his whole being was maturing like fine wine. One then has to imagine him as an old man, shuffling down to the dining area, Seppo challenging him, and Tokusan, without a word, turning around and shuffling off back to his room. If we can picture this act several questions come to mind. What is Seppo up to? Is he just being egoistic and rude? Is he thoughtless, or is he challenging Tokusan, "Hey, show me your Zen"?

We also have to wonder about the next act. Seppo tells Ganto about what happened. Was he bragging, saying that he caught the old man out in dharma combat? Ganto seems to think so and makes the comment that Tokusan doesn't know the last word of Zen. Ganto was probably fully awakened at this time, so other questions come to mind: why does he side with Seppo? what is the last word of Zen? how is it that a renowned teacher such as Tokusan does not know it?

Then in the final act Tokusan gives a talk like no other, and Ganto declares that he has truly grasped the last word of Zen.

Let us return to the first act to ask what was in Tokusan's mind when he returned to his room. Most of us, if we had been rudely treated and scolded by someone much younger than ourselves and lower in the hierarchy, would have retreated bearing a lot of resentful thoughts, "How dare he speak to me like that, I should never have made him head cook, he's too cocky. I should be able to be served when I want." Would this be how it was with Tokusan? Or would he have controlled these thoughts, kept his mind aloof, and have refused to be moved by Seppo? Or perhaps he would have flowed out love and compassion toward Seppo, hoping in this way to help him overcome his ignorance. What would you have done, reader?

Who *is* Tokusan, or more importantly, who are you? In the *Diamond Sutra* it is said:

> *All living beings are brought to Full Awakening by me.*
> *Yet when an uncountable number of beings have been*
> *liberated, no being has been liberated. Why is this? It*
> *is because no Bodhisattva who is a real Bodhisattva*
> *cherishes the idea of an "I," an ego-entity, a personali-*
> *ty, a being or a separated individuality.*

The study of Buddhism, Dogen pronounced, is the study of the self. To study the self one must forget the self. But how is one to forget the self, which is so omnipresent? How many times during a day does one use the word "I," how often do we think it? All our values have their origin in I. Everything is evaluated in terms of I: if we heard 100,000 people were killed in China we would be shocked, we would be equally shocked if we heard that 10,000 were killed in Europe or 1,000 in the next province or state. How shocked we would be if a hundred were killed in the town we live in or ten in the same street. But none of this would be as devastating as one person being killed in our own house. To forget I seems impossible unless we realize that I is not something after all.

A Japanese haiku says:

No one
walks this path
This autumn evening.

No one walked back to Tokusan's room. Who, or what, is this no one? What does Buddha mean when he says, "No Bodhisattva who is a real Bodhisattva cherishes the idea of an 'I'"? To know the answer to this directly, without thoughts or words, is to forget the self, to be no one. It is also to become Tokusan as he goes back to his room. To think about this, to understand it, is of no use, any more than eating a menu is of use in satisfying hunger.

Ganto says that Tokusan does not know the last word of Zen. What is this word, what is any word? Some think it is a label that is stuck on things, and that our practice is simply to unstick the labels. But words are magic. In Genesis is says, "God said 'Let there be light.'" God *said* this, or perhaps, as Leonard Bernstein once noted, "God sang it." But either way it was speaking the word that was the generative act. Again, in the New Testament it says, "In the beginning was the Word." The Jewish Cabala says that the world was created by ten utterances. Again, the word. Unfortunately, we have become swamped with words from newspapers, journals, books, advertisements, films, and lectures; they are now so cheap we throw them away by the millions. But even so, we have lost the real word, the live word, and so live in a twilight world. If words bring worlds into being, what brings words into being? How could we name that? Dogen exhorted his monks to think the unthinkable. It is the unthinkable that thinks and the unspeakable that speaks. One must say the last word without opening the mouth, and to know this word one must have already gone beyond anything.

A monk said to another monk, "I went to my teacher with nothing and I left with nothing." The second monk asked, "Why did you go to your teacher then?" The first replied, "How else would I know that I went with nothing and left with nothing?"

"Do you not approve of my teaching?" asked Tokusan, and Ganto whispered something to him. Tokusan would have taught the *Diamond Sutra*. Is it possible that Ganto would have disapproved of that? The *Diamond Sutra*

is one of the principal texts of Zen Buddhists. That is why
we have introduced excerpts and suggested that you read
them. But what is it really teaching and how is one to understand it?

Emperor Wu, the one who entertained Bodhidharma,
once invited Fu Daishi, a very famous lay practicer of Zen,
to lecture on the *Diamond Sutra*. For the occasion the
emperor invited the lords and ladies of the surrounding dis-
trict to attend the lecture. In the 67th koan of the
Hekiganroku Engo describes what happened: "Fu Daishi
approached the lectern and struck it with his stick. He then
turned and left. The emperor was dumbfounded."

In the *Diamond Sutra* it also says:

> *Therefore, Subhuti, the Bodhisattva, the great being,*
> *should produce a thought of complete, right and per-*
> *fect enlightenment. Unsupported by form should a*
> *thought be produced, unsupported by sounds, smells,*
> *tastes, or mind objects should a thought be produced,*
> *unsupported by dharmas should a thought be pro-*
> *duced, unsupported by anything should a thought be*
> *produced. A Bodhisattva should* arouse the mind with-
> out resting it upon anything.

What was the talk that Tokusan gave to his monks
that so pleased Ganto? Perhaps the following dialogue that
Hyakujo had with some dharma masters, the university pro-
fessors of his day, will give some help.

The dharma masters asked him, "Master, what dharma do you teach to liberate others?" Hyakujo replied, "This
poor monk has no teaching by which to liberate others."
The dharma masters exclaimed, "All Zen masters are of the
same stuff!" So Hyakujo in his turn asked them, "What

dharma do you virtuous ones teach in order to liberate others?" The dharma masters responded, "The *Diamond Sutra*." Hyakujo then asked them how many times they had given this teaching and they replied, "Oh! More that twenty times." "Whose words are given in the *Diamond Sutra*?" asked Hyakujo. The masters were quite shocked by this and rejoined, "Master, you must be joking! Everyone knows that it was the Buddha who expounded it." Hyakujo then retorted, "Well, that sutra says, 'If someone states that the Tathagata expounds the dharma, he thereby slanders the Buddha! Such a man will never understand what I mean.' Now, if you say that it was not expounded by the Buddha, you belittle the sutra. Will you virtuous ones please let me see what you have to say to that?"

Did Tokusan give a talk?

With no bird singing
The mountain is yet more still.

—From *A Zen Forest,* translated by Sōiku Shigematsu

14 Nansen Cuts the Cat

*T*he monks of the Eastern and Western Zen halls
were once quarreling about a cat. Nansen held up
the cat and said, "You monks if you can say a word of Zen
I will spare the cat. If you can't I will cut it in two." No one
could answer so Nansen cut the cat in two.

In the evening, when Joshu returned, Nansen told him
what had happened. Right away Joshu took off his sandal,
put it on his head, and walked away. Nansen said, "If you
had been there I would have spared the cat."

Mumon's Comment

Tell me, what did Joshu mean when he put the sandal on his
head? If you can give a turning word on this, you will see
that Nansen's decree was carried out with good reason. If
not, watch out!

Mumon's Verse

Had Joshu been there,
He would have done the opposite;
When the sword is snatched away,
Even Nansen begs for his life.

Comments

We have already encountered the word of Zen in earlier koans. Gutei was called on by a nun to give a word of Zen, and Tokusan was accused of not knowing it. A word of Zen is a word that one speaks without opening the mouth. It was this word that Joshu gave after Nansen had recounted the story of cutting the cat in two.

The monks were quarreling about a cat. Probably some of them were saying it was theirs while others were claiming it as theirs. Nansen calls for a word of Zen.

What is a quarrel? Some people will quarrel over a cat,

others over land, others over an object, but essentially a quarrel is always over an *idea,* and basically an idea is a way of seeing something, sometimes a way of seeing the world or *weltanschauung.* With this world idea or world view I separate *my* world from *the* world. What is left out after the separation I believe is of no consequence. On the old maps, what was unknown was shown as the realm of demons and monsters and best avoided or, what amounts to the same thing, ignored.

A problem arises when I meet up with you: instead of one, unified whole world, two worlds stand opposed. The history of the human race and the rise and fall of cultures have this problem underlying them. Between us we divide what is fundamentally one living, shining whole into two, each claiming *the* world. Laws, mores, rules, rites, and rituals are all ways of rediscovering lost unity by transforming my world into our world. This defers the problem, but does not solve it. Instead of my world being opposed to your world, our world is now opposed to their world: our family, our clan, our tribe, our nation, our ideology, our world versus theirs.

It is our world because it is mine and, so I like to believe, you are prepared to accept that it is mine. But as far as you are concerned, it is ours because it is yours and, so you like to believe, I am prepared to accept that it is yours. Relations are so unstable because they are dependent both on my way of seeing things as well as on your way of seeing things. That means relations can disintegrate over quarrels about something so trivial as who owns a cat. Their fragility is also illustrated by the fact that they can be patched up by something as trivial as a table tennis game, as was the case with the quarrel between the United States and China in the Nixon era.

Nansen Cuts the Cat

It is only by trust that a stable world can be found. If trust has gone, what can take its place? Armies, police forces, national guards, and secret police; nothing can bring back unity that no longer has trust as its main support. But what is trust? What does it mean when I say to someone, "I trust you?" Substituting terms such as "having confidence," "having faith," and "being able to rely on" doesn't answer the question, it simply puts it in another guise. What is trust, or confidence, or faith?

This koan also appears in the *Hekiganroku*. In fact, it appears there as two koans. The first ends where Nansen cuts the cat; the second recounts Joshu's reaction, or perhaps it is better to say his action. In the introduction to the first koan Engo says, "Where the way of ideas can go no further, there you must put your attention; where explanation fails, there you must set your gaze." I think it was Paul who said something about faith being the substance of things unseen. That is so. Faith is the substance of all things, both seen and unseen, because *faith is in the seeing, in the knowing*. We can even say faith *is* knowing. Faith freezes into belief, and we lose our life when we have faith *in* God or Buddha or the ideology of the group. But alas, to say faith is knowing is to commit the very error that Nansen wants to correct in the monks. We cannot say what faith is, but we can say that when I set up my world, or our world against another's world, I kill the world. A word of Zen will heal the rift by showing the underlying reality of the world that the monks, by quarreling, are tearing in two. This is why Nansen called for a word of Zen, and when he could not get it from the monks he provided it for them.

But why kill the cat? This is one of the koans that people who fail to see the spirit of koans do not understand. I remember hearing a monk say, "Zen is not a game; you

must be ready to put your life on the line." The life we put
on the line is the life of ego, the life lived at the expense of
others.

Jesus said, "I bring not peace, but a sword." It was a
sword of death and resurrection. Did he not say, "Truly,
truly, I say unto you, unless a grain of wheat falls into the
earth and dies, it remains alone; but if it dies, it brings forth
much fruit. He who loves his life loses it"? Mumon says in
his commentary on Joshu's Mu! that once you have seen
into the koan, if you meet the Buddha you will kill the
Buddha; if you meet the patriarchs, you will kill the patriarchs. The Buddha and the patriarchs are what we value,
they make up the life that we must lose and are just so many
obstacles to one's work.

The reader might say, "I can understand why Jesus
said we must die in order to gain life everlasting, but what
about the cat? Why kill the cat? The cat is not me after all."
It is at that moment that the cat is killed. It is said that the
sword of prajna, the sword with which Nansen killed the
cat, is a sword that cuts not in two but in one. To allow the
Buddha to live is to have two worlds: the Buddha's world
and my world. To allow the cat to live is to have half a cat
in the world of the monks of the east wing and half in the
world of the west wing.

In the *Hekiganroku* Etcho says,

> *Lost in thought, the monks of both halls*
> *Waged war of attrition.*
> *Fortunately Nansen was there;*
> *His words and deeds were one.*
> *He cut the cat in two*
> *Beyond right and wrong.*

15 Tozan's Sixty Blows

*T*ozan came to learn from Ummon who asked him, "Where are you from?" "From Sato," Tozan replied. "Where were you during the summer?" "I was at the monastery of Hozu, south of the lake." Ummon asked again, "When did you leave there?" Tozan replied, "On the 25th of August." "I won't give you sixty blows," said Ummon.

The next day Tozan came to Ummon and queried, "Yesterday you said you would not give me sixty blows. Please, let me ask you, what did I do wrong?" "Oh you useless good-for-nothing!" shouted Ummon. "What is it that makes you wander about now west of the river, now south of the lake?" At that Tozan came to great awakening.

Mumon's Comment

All night long Tozan wallowed in the sea of yes and no and he could get nowhere. He reached a complete impasse. And when at last dawn broke, he went back to Ummon, and Ummon again gave him a picture book of Zen. Even though he was brought to awakening, Tozan could not be called brilliant.

Now, I want to ask you, should Tozan have been beaten or not? If you say yes then what you are saying is that the whole world should be beaten. If you say no then are you saying that Ummon is a fool and a bully? If you can really get to know the secret, you will be able to breathe the Zen spirit with the very mouth of Tozan.

Mumon's Verse

> *The lion has a roundabout way of teaching her cubs*:*
> *Intending to urge them on she pushes them away.*
> *Soon they redress themselves and charge back.*
> *Heedlessly he came back to Ummon but was check-*
>   *mated;*
> *The first arrow was only a scratch, but the second*
>   *went deep.*

Comment

Where are you from? It is an innocuous question. Most likely it would have been a usual one. In China, at that time many monks were wandering from monastery to monastery, some genuinely in search of a teacher for whom they could feel affinity and with whom they could settle down and work; others were wandering for the sake of wandering or because they couldn't settle down, or because they were running away from something. Where are you from? would have been a natural question, similar to what we often ask nowadays: what do you do? The answer helps us put the person in context. Suppose one were to answer, "Nothing." What sort of reaction would you have?

---

*It is said that three days after she gives birth to her cubs, a lioness will kick her beloved offspring from the precipice into an unfathomable valley. She cares for only those promising ones that scale the cliff, and deserts those that were not brave enough to do so.

Probably you would think in terms of unemployment, retirement, or laziness.

Tozan's answer was also natural: at the monastery of Hozu, south of the lake. So was his next answer in reply to being asked when he left there. Why then was Ummon so upset, saying, in effect, "You are not even worth the trouble of beating"?

Put yourself in Tozan's place. Just imagine you hear about a Zen center with an outstanding teacher and decide to go there, not by plane and taxi, but by walking. After great effort and not a little danger you finally arrive, knock on the door, somewhat nervous perhaps, certainly tired but also with a great deal of hope and eagerness. You are not invited in, but instead, even before you can properly introduce yourself, you are asked, "Where are you from?" You reply, perhaps with a polite smile. "When did you leave there?" "Two weeks ago." All of a sudden this fellow in front of you drops on you like an avalanche of wet snow off a roof, yelling at you to clear off, not to waste his time, calling you names and so on. What would be your reaction? Anger? Bewilderment? Confusion? Fear at what he'll do next? Profound disappointment? Guilt? Probably all of these and more.

The koan simply continues with Tozan going to Ummon the next day and asking where he was at fault. But what it leaves out is what happens between his leaving Ummon and his returning. Most of us, let us confess, would have turned on our heel and left for good, probably cursing Ummon for being an inconsiderate dolt, an ignorant fool, and any other name we could find handy. But Tozan did not. Why not? This is the entry into the koan. Something must have penetrated through to Tozan in the midst of that tirade. But what?

A similar situation unfolds in the following story. A monk asked Rinzai, "What is a person of no rank?" Rinzai got down from his meditation seat, grabbed the monk by the front of his robe, hit him a couple of times around the face, and pushed him away crying, "What a useless bit of garbage is this man of no rank!" Then somebody said to the monk, "Why don't you bow?" The monk came to awakening.

Confused, bewildered, lost, yet in the midst of it all he comes to awakening. When Joshu was asked, "When the mountains close in on you on every side from all four directions, what then?", he answered, "It is the pathless that is Joshu!" When one is confused, depressed, and lost, what then? It is the pathless that is Joshu.

In a few words Mumon sums up the Great Work. He says, "All night long Tozan wallowed in the sea of yes and no and he could get nowhere. He reached a complete impasse." If one can understand why Tozan did not leave Ummon, one will also understand what Mumon means by wallowing all night in yes and no.

The British philosopher F.H. Bradley was more prolix but perhaps more descriptive when he wrote,

> *The shades nowhere speak without blood and the ghosts of Metaphysic accept no substitute. They reveal themselves only to that victim whose life they have drained, and, to converse with shadows he himself must become a shadow.*
>
> *The person whose nature is such that by one path alone his/her desire will reach consummation will try to find it on that path whatever it might be and whatever the world thinks of it; and, if he does not, he is*

contemptible. Self-sacrifice is too often the "great"
sacrifice of trade, the giving cheap what is worth noth-
ing. To know what one wants, and to scruple at no
means that will get it, may be a harder self-surrender.[5]

Tozan passed through the dark night of the soul, a
dark night through which any aspirant to the truth must
pass. Without having hungered and thirsted after righteousness, as Jesus would say, without having emptied oneself of
all, without having touched bottom, one will not be filled. A
quotation from Nisargadatta puts it all in a nutshell:
"Whatever name you give it: will or steady purpose or one
pointedness of mind, you come back to earnestness, sincerity, honesty. When you are in dead earnest you bend every
incident, every second of your life to your purpose. You do
not waste time and energy on other things, you are totally
dedicated, call it will or love or plain honesty. We are complex beings at war within and without. We contradict ourselves all the time undoing the work of today the work of
yesterday. No wonder we are stuck. A little integrity would
make a lot of difference."[6]

One of the most inspiring stories about someone who
came to awakening is told by Hsu Yun in his autobiography. Hsu Yun died in the 1950s at the age of about one
hundred and thirty. He had been badly abused by the Red
Guard in China some time before and never fully recovered
from his beating. He tells of his awakening that occurred
when he was already well past fifty years of age.

He was on his way to a *sesshin* (Zen Buddhist retreat),
walking along a river swollen from recent rains, when he
slipped and fell into the water. He said he was "bobbing in
the water for one day and one night until I drifted to the

[5] Quoted by Sushil Kumar Saxena in *Studies in the Metaphysics of Bradley.*
(New York: Allen and Unwin, 1967).

[6] From *I Am That.*

Ts'ai Shih jetty where a fisherman caught me in his net." He was bleeding profusely from every orifice, but when he had recovered sufficiently he continued on to the monastery for the sesshin. The abbot of the monastery asked him to do some work in preparation for the sesshin, but Hsu Yun was so exhausted that he had to refuse. According to the rules of the monastery, to refuse a request from the abbot was considered to be an affront to the whole community; Hsu Yun was judged guilty of this offense and was punished with a wooden stick. This aggravated his condition and he bled continuously. "Waiting for my end, I sat firmly in the meditation hall day and night with increasing zeal. In the purity of my singleness of mind, I forgot all about my body." Twenty days later his infirmities vanished completely. One night, well into the retreat, he was being served tea when the server clumsily poured hot water on to his hand and scalded it. The shock caused Hsu Yun to drop the cup and it broke. At that moment he came to deep awakening.

The determination and courage that were required to sit in the face of what seemed certain death, was great. To continue after he had virtually been rejected by the community, to refuse to justify himself or explain, and so dissipate his energy to no avail, demanded earnestness, sincerity, honesty. Kierkegaard, the Danish philosopher, says "purity of heart is to will one thing." In Hsu Yun's case, and in Tozan's too, it would have been to will *no-thing*. Tozan would not have been able to will one thing because he did not know what to will.

As Mumon noted, Tozan reached a complete impasse. He was like a rat in a bamboo tube, to use Hakuin's expression. He could not go forward and he could not go back.

But he could not stay where he was. He returned to Ummon and was again abused. But this time the ice castle shattered, Tozan had nowhere to go. His state of mind at that moment could be expressed by:

For years I suffered in the snow and frost;
but now I am startled at pussy willows falling.

How would you answer the question, where are you from? Mumon gives a valuable clue in his commentary by asking whether or not Tozan should have been beaten. "If you say yes then what you are saying is the whole world should be beaten. If you say no then are you saying that Ummon is a fool and a bully?" Why should the whole world be beaten if Tozan is to be beaten, and what has this to do with the question?

The words of a woman who probably had no knowledge or experience of Zen give a clue: "I was standing alone on the edge of a low cliff overlooking a small valley leading to the sea. It was late afternoon or early evening and there were birds swooping in the sky—possibly swallows. Suddenly my mind 'felt' as though it had changed gear or switched into another view of things. I still saw the birds and everything around me, but instead of standing looking at them, I *was* them and they were me. I was also the sea and the sound of the sea and the grass and the sky. Everything and I were the same, all one . . . I was filled, swamped with happiness and peace. Everything was *right*. I do not know how long it lasted, probably a second or two. I am told that it is an early stage of awareness of a desperate need for at-one-ment, to which those who think about these things are striving."

Koans: Fifteen

Zen master Bunan, upon coming to awakening, wrote this poem:

> The moon's the same old moon
> The flowers are just as they were
> Yet now I am
> The thingness of things.

16 Ummon's "The World is Vast and Wide"

*U*mmon said, "The world is vast and wide; why do you put on your seven-piece robe at the sound of the bell?"

Mumon's Comment

In general, learning the Way and practicing Zen means to avoid getting attached to sounds and forms. Though by hearing a sound one may come to awakening, or from seeing the form of an object the mind may be enlightened, nevertheless this is the ordinary way of things. Especially you Zen monks do not understand how to guide sound, use form, see clearly the value of each thing, each activity of the mind. But though this is so, just tell me! Does the sound come to the ear or does the ear go to the sound? But when sound and silence are both forgotten, what can you say of this state? If you listen with your ear, it is truly hard, but if you listen with your eye, then you begin to hear properly.

Koans: Sixteen

Mumon's Verse

> *If you are enlightened, all things are as though of one family,*
> *But if not, everything is separate and disconnected.*
> *If you are not enlightened [it makes no difference because] all things are as of one family.*
> *And if you are enlightened; [it also makes no difference because] every single thing is different from everything else.*

Comment

Picture a monastery first thing in the morning. From some distance away in the mist a bell rings. A monk gets out of bed and, as is his custom, puts on his robe. Someone asks, "The world is vast and wide. Why do you put on your robe?"

I am often asked similar questions: Why do you chant and bow down to Buddha? Why do you spend so much time in meditation? Aren't Zen practices beyond all form? Rituals and ceremonies at the Montreal Zen Center are minimal because we have always thought they should arise out of the moment and not be imposed from without. Japanese rituals are wonderful to behold as are the robes and paraphernalia worn by the monks and priests. All of them arose out of centuries of practice and the awakening of many people in Japan. For us in the West to adopt these as our own without having yet paid their price would be like cultural theft. But to have no ritual at all seems too bare, too bald, and the danger always lurks that a cult of the personality of the leader could develop. Therefore we maintain a few ceremonies and chants: the four vows, the chant in praise of zazen, chanting the *Prajnaparamita Hridaya* and the three prostrations. We also wear robes, but for practical rather than ceremonial reasons. Although we have so little ritual, people still ask, why have rituals at all?

In this koan, however, is buried a more serious question, on which in turn the question about rituals stands: "Why do zazen? Why submit yourself to any kind of discipline? Is not Zen the way of the Great Liberation?"

I remember attending a talk many years ago given by a Westerner who had spent a few months in a Buddhist monastery in the Far East. Because in those few months he had not learned any better, he was still confusing arbitrary behavior with freedom. He was giving his talk standing behind a small table on which someone had thoughtfully put a jug of water with a glass on a small wooden tray. The table was covered with a cloth, and it was obvious someone had arranged it all with respect. Somewhere along in his talk the man suddenly avowed, "Look I am free! free from all restraint!" and, to punctuate his remark, he seized hold of the table and with one flip of his hand sent table, cloth, jug, water, and glass flying. It would be difficult to find a better example of what Zen does *not* mean by freedom. Unfortunately, it has been the *apparent* anarchistic behavior, the zany behavior of some Zen monks, that has appealed to the West along with the *apparent* anti-intellectual, anti-reason of Zen. The word apparent is emphasized for good reason. Even so, this "crazy" Zen has been a good seller and some people from Asia have been quick to pick up on its commercial possibilities, to say nothing of the licentiousness they can practice in its name.

This same craze for freedom haunts modern art. The belief that the artist is free when he has no restraints is a fallacy. As Hubert Benoit pointed out in his book *The Supreme Doctrine*, "freedom is total determinism."

Why do anything? Sometimes this question haunts people in another way. They find everything they do vaguely pointless. They see the point but not the *point*, and without that point the world becomes a wasteland.

Ummon's question begins with, "The world is vast and wide." One is reminded of Bodhidharma's "vast emptiness and nothing that can be called holy." Or, in terms of what we are saying here, vast emptiness with nothing that can be called ultimately meaningful. Why then put on your robe, why then sit on the meditation mat? What is the point? To answer this we must see into vast emptiness.

Mumon seems to be saying something similar to Bodhidharma when he remarks, "In general, learning the way and practicing Zen means to avoid getting attached to sounds and forms." Is not chanting an attachment to sound, is not zazen attachment to form? He goes on: "You Zen monks do not understand how to guide sound, use form, see clearly the value of each thing, each activity of the mind. . . . Does the sound come to the ear or does the ear go to the sound?"

Listen to a bird singing. The bird is over there, in that tree, opening its mouth and giving forth. Without the bird no singing occurs. You are over here listening. Without your listening, *for you* no sound occurs. Now listen carefully and ask yourself Mumon's question, which can be phrased: where does the hearing begin and the sound end. Where does the sound begin and the hearing end? Please do not *think* about this, but rather address the sound directly.

You could try the same experiment with touch. Feel the page; once again, on the face of it, two things come together: the page which is "out there" and the feeling which is "in here." Put another way, apparently self and other come together. In order to be able really to feel the page it is best to close the eyes and just let the hand pass over the paper. Where does the feeling end and the paper begin?

Buddha said, "The sound of the bell continues during a space of time; how do we become conscious of it? Does the sound come from the ear, or does the ear go to the sound? If it does not go [one way or the other] there is no hearing. For this reason, it must be understood that *neither hearing nor sound is special* (my emphasis). We mistakenly put hearing and sound in two different places. *Originally it is not a matter of cause and effect*" (my emphasis).

In the same way we put the sound of the bell and dressing oneself in the seven-piece robe in two places; one the cause, we say, the other the effect. Can you see what this means? If not, try the exercise again of feeling the page, and this time remember it is important to let go of all thought. Are there two or is there only one? The *Surangama Sutra* from which all of this comes tells us, "Even in dreams when all thinking has become quiescent, the hearing nature is still alert."

I must warn you that the exercise can only give you a picture. If you want to look through the window you must ask yourself, what "the way is vast and wide" means. See into this and you will see that all things are as though one family. If you don't, you will be something in a world of somethings, a fragmented world lacking coherence and point. Even if you do not see into it, the world is still one coherent whole, but it is "my" world, circumscribed by fear and aggression, defended against the encroachment of the "unknown" and "unconscious" forces by greed and desire. On the other hand, if you see into it, everything is as it is. In

Zen it is said, "Tall bamboos are tall; short bamboos are short."

Before leaving this koan, when a bird sings, where are you? See into this and you will know why it is that when the bell rings you put on your seven-piece robe.

17 The National Teacher Calls Three Times

*T*he National teacher called his attendant three
times, and the attendant responded three times.
The National teacher mourned, "I have always been afraid I
was letting you down, but in fact it was you who were letting me down."

Mumon's Comment

The National teacher called three times and his tongue fell
to the ground. The attendant responded brilliantly three
times. The National teacher was old and lonely; he held the
cow's head and tried to make it eat grass. The attendant was
not interested; even delicious food has no attraction for one
who is full.

Tell me, who was letting whom down and when?
When the country is flourishing, talent is prized. When the
home is wealthy, the children are proud.

Koans: Seventeen

Mumon's Verse

He carried an iron yoke with no hole
And left a curse to trouble his descendants.
If you want to hold up the gate and the doors,
You must climb a mountain of swords with bare feet.

Comment

This is a third in a trio of koans, of which the first is Wakuan's Beard, the second, Zuigan Calls the Master. All koans are windows onto true nature, which is essentially whole, One. We most often think of One as passive, even abstract. As an abstraction, One is what is left after all other attributes have been stripped away. We fail to appreciate that Oneness is not at all passive but intensely active, intensely dynamic. One should not be seen as a noun but as a verb; One is going toward One in an irresistible manner and doing so by way of One. Perhaps instead of One, we should refer to *dynamic unity*.

This dynamic nature of unity is expressed in Zen by insistence on *demonstrating* truth and not simply talking about it. In the introduction we mentioned the two aspects of koans, essential and functional. We spoke of the koan in which a master and disciple are working, hoeing a field, and the disciple asks the master, "What is it?" The master simply stands still and the disciple says, "You have the essence, but not the function." The master says, "O.K. What is it?" and the disciple goes on hoeing. Unless we see into this dynamic essential aspect of unity we can never "understand" the shouting, banging, and hitting of the Zen masters. The Kwatz! that Rinzai yells out is pure dynamism.

But if One is basic, where does the Other come from? Or more immediately, in terms of these three koans; if, as

The National Teacher Calls Three Times

Buddha said, "Throughout Heaven and Earth I alone am the honored One," where do *you* come in? This is a problem that has taxed the minds of a legion of philosophers. One response is to say the world is but a dream I am dreaming, which is fine for me but not so hot for you. To bring you into the picture some teachers introduce the "overself" or "cosmic consciousness": we are all part of one great mind. But if we invent a cosmic consciousness we simply complicate the question because we now have three in the equation, me, you, and cosmic consciousness.

Both these responses—the world is a dream and the idea of an "overself"—slip into many Zen talks and writings in the name of Buddha nature or self nature. But let us not forget that when the monk asked Joshu whether a dog has Buddha nature, Joshu replied, "No!"

These three koans, each in its own way, address the question, "Where do you fit into the picture?" or, "If I am dynamic unity, where does the Other come in?"

The National teacher calls his attendant. To call someone naturally implies, "I am over here, you are over there." The attendant would have been in his room, perhaps meditating, reading, or doing whatever monks do in their off hours. The master wants something and calls out, "Attendant!" The attendant gets up and runs to the master's room, "Yes? what do you want?" This must have been a daily occurrence. Then one day the master calls *three* times. What the koan doesn't say is what happens between the attendant responding and the master calling for him again. Or was there anything between?

Let us be the attendant. The master calls once; this is normal. He calls twice; well, perhaps he needs company. But three times! That's odd, I wonder what's the matter with the old boy? Mumon asks a similar question: "Who is letting whom down and when?" But before we can answer that question we have to ask who is the master and who the attendant? This is the very same question we asked overtly with Zuigan and implicitly with Wakuan.

Ask yourself, "Who am I?" or "What am I?" To enter into this question one must ask it in all of its concreteness, all of its thereness, or hereness. Are you something? Are you a sensation, an emotion, a thought? Obviously not; all of these come and go, but they come and go in reference to *you*. You will not find yourself even in consciousness because each night you put consciousness on one side and go to sleep. So what are you? You are not nothing; nothing is a pure abstraction. We already tackled that question in Keitchu's wheel. So who or what are you? It is only through the door of yourself that you will come to the Other but this is not to say the Other is a projection or a dream; nor does it mean you are the dreamer.

The master said, "I thought I was letting you down." This is always a fear that a teacher has when guiding others in Zen. The more one says the more one complicates the issue, and to say this is to complicate it even more. Harada Roshi said that during the time he was a teacher he was selling water by the river. The problem is that by taking it out of the river and putting it into a container one has already polluted it. All that a teacher can do is to call out to the student. But even this is too much; already one has made waves where there is no wind. If I call you, I have made something of you. Nothing needs to be done.

Most students try to *understand* the call of the master. They ask themselves why the teacher is calling, what the teacher means, why he is calling loudly or softly, and so on.

And so the teacher is constrained to call again, digging deeper into the wound in the flesh that would be otherwise healthy. But the good student just lets the master talk, lets him call. He does not need anything, not even to tell the teacher he does not need anything. It is no longer a case of the master calling the student but of the student calling the master. After all, as we have already asked, who is the teacher, who the student?

With respect to this koan, a monk asked Hogen, "What is the meaning of the National teacher's calling the attendant?" Hogen replied, "Ask me some other time." But when would be an appropriate time?

Joshu said in reply to the same question, "It is like a man writing in the dark; the letters are not quite right but they are legible." Even when letting the student down the meaning of the master is still there.

18 Tozan's Three Pounds of Flax

A monk asked Tozan, "What is Buddha?" He replied, "Three pounds of flax."

Mumon's Comment

Old Tozan is rather like a clam; scarcely opening the two halves of the shell, it shows its liver and intestines. But though this may be so, just say where can we see Tozan?

Mumon's Verse

> "Three pounds of flax"—*without a thought, sponta-*
> *neously it comes out.*
> *The words and meaning are one, indivisibly so.*
> *Anyone who explains this and that, yes and no, the*
> *relative and the absolute,*
> *Is himself only a relative person.*

Comment

A monk asked Tozan, "What is Buddha?" But what kind of monk? It is imperative that we ask this question, for without seeing clearly that it was no ordinary monk, we fail to see that Tozan's answer was no ordinary answer. What is Buddha?

The fundamental sin of Buddhism is ignorance. Actually, it is a *klesa* rather than a sin. A klesa is that which brings suffering to oneself and to others, and basic to all klesas is ignorance. Sin, on the other hand, is to break the rules, to disobey God's commandments. If one examines the commandments carefully, one can see they are all designed to help us avoid causing pain to others and so ultimately to ourselves.

Two other klesas are derived immediately from ignorance: the first is anger, aggression, or hate; the second is greed, envy, or jealousy.

What is ignorance? It is not lack of information or of education. Indeed, additional information, more education can often simply deepen the klesa of ignorance. The secret of ignorance lies in the word itself, because it contains the verb "to ignore." We have to ask ourselves what it is that we ignore. Ignore means to avoid, to turn away from, to turn one's back on. But deeper still it means "to not-know."

It is fundamental to Buddhism that we are whole and complete. We lack nothing. Our true nature is *knowing*. Buddha is associated with Bodhi, which means light or knowing. Why then do we suffer, or, more to the point here, from where does ignorance come? This is really the most basic question that we can ask in Zen practice. It was this question that drove Dogen deeper and deeper into himself.

When I give workshops and talk about the first noble

truth, that suffering is basic to life, someone usually objects and says this is pessimistic, that life is wonderful, beautiful, that happiness is the true nature of the human being. They are of course right—Buddha is right, the people who object are right. Life is basically suffering, yet it is basically happiness. There is a story of a court case in which the counsel for the prosecution made his case and the judge said, "You are right!" The counsel for the defense made his case and the judge said, "You are right!" Then the clerk of the court got up, somewhat exasperated and said, "But my Lord, they can't both be right!" And the judge said, "You are right!"

Ignorance arises when we turn our back on the whole in favor of some part and claim that this part is the whole. In the West we call it idolatry. We surrender all-knowing, our true nature, in favor of knowing *something* that we claim is the whole. Money, fame, love, knowledge, and success are the idols of our time, and in our search for them we forget our true home.

And so we start to see the trap into which the monk is trying to push Tozan: Buddha is wholeness or completeness; how is Tozan to reply without falling into the klesa of ignorance, without committing idolatry? Because the monk is awake, Tozan cannot say Buddha is this or that, he cannot give explanations; the monk knows that Buddha is not this or that, and that explanations are so many bubbles of air. As Mumon declares in his verse: the one "who explains this and that, yes and no, the relative and absolute is himself only a relative person."

Every time the question "what is Buddha?" is asked, this trap is baited, and each time a master replies he says something fundamental about Buddha without falling into the trap. How does Tozan manage to do this?

Tozan's Three Pounds of Flax

One has to imagine Tozan working with his monks. He weighs flax into three-pound bundles, and the monks tie up the bundles and store them. He is totally one with his work. Then a new monk comes from nowhere and shoots this question at Tozan, who says, "Three pounds of flax."

To say that three pounds of flax is Buddha, and therefore everything else is not, is surely idolatry. A master once spat on a Buddha figure. The master of the temple was horrified and rushed over shouting, "What are you doing, that's the Buddha you are spitting on!" The master looked around saying, "Well then, show me what is not the Buddha and I'll spit there."

This is precisely the trap that Tozan avoided. But how did he say, "Three pounds of flax?" This is the crux of the issue. Did he thrust three pounds of flax out and say, "Three pounds of flax!"? Mumon, in his commentary, gives a clue, "Old Tozan is rather like a clam; scarcely opening the two halves of the shell, it shows its liver and the intestines." A Zen couplet sums up the whole situation:

She goes into the lake without making a ripple,
She goes into the forest without disturbing a blade
  of grass.

19 Ordinary Mind Is the Way

*J*oshu asked Nansen, *"What is the Way?" Nansen answered, "Ordinary mind is the Way." "How do you get on to it?" "The more you try to get on to it, the more you push it away." "How do you know you are on the Way?" "The Way has nothing to do with knowledge, but it is not not-knowing. Knowledge is illusory, not-knowing, lack of discrimination. It is like vast space. Where is there room for this and that, is and is not?"*

Upon this Joshu came to sudden awakening.

Mumon's Comment

Joshu suddenly brought up the question to Nansen, who explained it, but even though the ice dissolves, the drain nevertheless is blocked up. Even though Joshu has come to awakening, he must work at it for another thirty years before he can get it completely.

Ordinary Mind is the Way

Mumon's Verse

In spring, the flowers;
In summer, cool breezes;
In autumn, the moon;
The snow in winter.
If the mind is not clouded by unnecessary things,
This day is a happy day in human life.

Comment

One of the things we emphasize at the Montreal Zen Center is that we do not need a special mind with which to practice Zen. We must always start where we are. Some people who have read the awakening stories of others try hard to "get into" their practice, they make great efforts and tense the body and squeeze the mind. But all that one gets into is the effort to get into practice. A lot of this effort is drama, and one could say the less faith one has the more drama will be necessary. At some centers the stick is used in an unmerciful way; at others, participants at a retreat are forbidden to sleep for the week, with the aim of pushing people into a state of desperation so they will break through their initial koans. This may well bring about insight for some people, but even for them, from the point of view of bringing about a transformation of the whole person, such a way is often unproductive. I have worked with people who have undergone this kind of treatment and found most are stuck in a knee-jerk, conditioned response to koans, and sometimes it has taken years to undo the harm they have suffered in this way.

Spiritual work comes out of a need for the truth. We all know the truth because we are the truth. Indeed, it is because we are the truth that we seek the truth, it is because we are one and whole that we seek unity. As St. Augustine said, "If you had not already found me, you would not be seeking me." It is because we are whole that we suffer. Our problem is we have turned our back on the truth to search for its reflection in experience. Hakuin painted a picture of a monkey trying to fish the reflection of the moon from out of the water, which illustrates our plight very well.

We seek unity in what we call happiness, success,

possessions, power, and so on, but it always seems to elude us, as indeed it must, as we can never find truth in reflections. But even though we have turned our back on it, the truth is always there. To find it we have to let go of reflections and turn around. If we do this it will seem we are letting go of all we hold dear: our values, hopes, and accomplishments. Even meaning itself will have to be sacrificed. It will seem as though we are committing spiritual suicide. Where can we find the strength to do this?

It is in being honest, accepting that our hopes, dreams, and so on mask the deep anguish of being lost, away from home. It is the anguish that comes from being alive. Practice is having the courage to be one with it. As the "Hymn of Jesus" says, "If you knew how to suffer, you would have the power not to suffer."

Perhaps suffering is too heavy a word. What we are talking about is that feeling of life not being quite right, that something vital in our life is seeping away, wasting away. This is the suffering that comes from knowing we are being called, but being unable to give a face or form to what is calling. Gurdjieff speaks of the "great evil inner god self calming," and it is this God who builds between us and the world buffers of dreams of glory and hopes for the impossible. Striving after awakening, putting effort into our practice, being part of a spiritual team that is really going places, all this builds wonderful buffers. The Way is to see these buffers for what they are. It is to live in the moment, to be where one is, and not wish to move from that spot. This, in the words of the hymn, is knowing how to suffer.

Practice can be likened to being out camping, wanting to light a fire with only one match and with the available fuel slightly wet: first one seeks a few of the drier leaves and lights them; then one carefully pulls a few other leaves on top, then a few more leaves; then one adds a few twigs, then bigger twigs. It then becomes possible to put on small branches, then bigger branches, and, before you know where you are, a blazing fire springs up, big enough to burn down a whole forest.

To try to set light to the big branches and so have a blazing fire right away simply causes the match to go out. The New Testament contains a story about the widow's mite. A mite was worth about a cent. It was all she had and she gave it. This mite was as valuable as the fortune that another richer person could give. The key to practice is *honesty*, and yet if one is honest one knows how difficult it is to be honest. And if one is honest, one knows one is striving to be special, unique, and that by fair means or foul one must rise above, transcend, go beyond, ordinary mind. The suffering of practice is to surrender this wish and to face whatever the wish has been hiding.

One of my favorite Zen stories is about a messenger of a Chinese emperor who was searching for a particular Zen master. He had searched everywhere without success until one day he came to a village, and one of the villagers said, "Yes, I know him. He lives under the bridge with the beggars." "With the beggars!" exclaimed the messenger, "How will I ever recognize him?" "Oh that's easy, he loves melons. Take a melon with you, and the one who grabs it first will be the master you are looking for."

Ordinary mind is the way. Someone, commenting on this koan, said that ordinary mind means the mind cleared of all its contradictions. But then Joshu would have had to ask, "How does one get rid of one's contradictions?" Ordinary mind is the mind of ambition, greed and envy,

love and fear, hate and aggression, compassion and gratitude, all confused and mixed up. Self-confidence and arrogance mixed with modesty and self-deprecation, indistin-
guishable one from the other. One thinks of St. Paul who
said, "That which I would not, that I do; that which I
would, that I do not." This could well be the anthem of
ordinary mind.

But, asks Joshu, how do we get on the Way? Once we
look upon ordinary mind as the Way, it most likely will no
longer be ordinary mind and no longer the Way. To see
ordinary mind as the Way one must be like a thief in the
night: one disturbs nothing as one moves in. So how are we
to know that we are on the Way if every move that we make
takes us away from it? To know is to grasp, to grasp is to
freeze. But simply to sit with a blank mind happily not
knowing is of no use either. This is the ultimate double
bind.

Ummon once gave a talk in which he said: "This work
that you do in the zendo is the most important work, but
should you come to some awakening, this will simply be due
to what you already are. When you hear about Zen you go
off searching for it everywhere, but in so doing you go farther and farther from the truth. Does this mean that one
should not search for the truth? Well, what other way is
there other than one of these two? The way of truth which
was transmitted by our ancestors? Be careful!"

In the koan, Nansen suddenly swings right around, "It
is like vast space." This is the pivot of the koan. In this lies
its bite. On the one hand he is saying that ordinary mind is
the Way, ordinary mind in all its darkness and confusion, all
its claustrophobic narrowness. On the other he says, "It is
like vast space. Where is there room for this and that, is and

is not?" Is he now contradicting himself? Is he saying after all the Way is not ordinary mind but vast space? That would make nonsense of the koan and of Nansen. How are we to understand this sudden change of direction of Nansen's? Mumon sums it all up beautifully in his verse:

> *In spring, the flowers,*
> *In summer, cool breezes;*
> *In autumn, the moon.*
> *The snow in winter.*
> *If the mind is not clouded with unnecessary things,*
> *This day is a happy day in human life.*

Joshu, later in his life, when he had thoroughly digested the truth he had stumbled over, said, "When I am hungry I eat, when I am tired I sleep."

Mumon's comment, "Even though Joshu has come to awakening he must work at it for another thirty years before he can get it completely" is too important for us not to address. To be able to say "When I am hungry I eat and when I am tired I sleep" requires years of practice to see into, and further years of practice to do. People often misunderstand the real meaning of awakening, thinking that on awakening, either the person is necessarily like Buddha with all the wisdom, compassion, and self-control of Buddha, or it is just another experience that, like all experiences, comes and goes. Neither view is right.

Zen master Isan gives us some insight into the thirty years of work that Joshu did after his awakening. He says, "If one is truly awakened and has realized true nature, and knows it for oneself, in such a case one is actually no longer tied to the poles of practice. But usually, even though the original mind has been awakened through practice, so one comes suddenly to awakening in one's very knowing reason, yet there still remains the inertia of habit, formed since the beginning of time, which cannot be totally got rid of at a stroke. Such a person must be taught to cut off completely the stream of habitual ideas and views caused by the still operative karmas. This process of purification is practice. I don't say one must follow a special hard and fast discipline. All one needs to know is the general direction practice must take. What you are told must first be accepted by your reason; and when your mind is deepened and becomes subtle in a way that cannot be described your mind will of its own spontaneity becomes comprehensive and bright, never to relapse into the state of doubt and delusion."

20 The Man of Great Strength

*S*hogen Osho asked, *"Why is it a man of great
strength does not lift his legs?"* And he also said,
"He does not speak with his tongue."

Mumon's Comment
It must be said Shogen shows us all his stomach and
intestines. But alas, no one can appreciate him! And even if
someone can appreciate him, let him come to me, and I'll
beat him severely. Why? If you want to find pure gold, you
must see it through fire.

Mumon's Verse

> *Lifting his leg, he kicks up the scented ocean;*
> *Lowering his head, he looks down on the highest*
>   *heaven.*

The Man of Great Strength

His body is so big there is no where to put it—
Now, somebody write the last line here.

Comment

Who is the man of great strength, or the woman of great strength? In the *Prajnaparamita* it speaks of

The Bodhisattva
holding to nothing whatever
who is freed from delusive ignorance
and rid of the fear bred by it.

We are like giants of great power who, with the left hand, push down our right hand with all our strength and, at the same time, push up the left hand with our right hand, also with all of our strength. That is why we take so long to come to awakening. We are told to let go, and we think this means push down harder or push up harder; we feel something must triumph, even if it is just some gesture of relaxation. The master exhorts us to let go of our hold on the cliff, to "hold on to nothing whatever." But our holding on is not some innocuous action; it is a matter of life and death.

In the introduction we quoted:

Empty-handed I carry the hoe.
Walking I ride the water buffalo.
The bridge across which I walk flows,
The stream is still.

This is the poem of a man of great strength.

On one occasion I was going to the airport to catch a plane. This was quite a long time ago when I was very much a man of the world. At the time I thought one mark of such a man of the world was that he did not wait around for planes but arrived at the airport at the last moment and casually strolled onto the plane. Unfortunately, this time the man of the world had left it just a little too long, and it was going to be touch and go whether or not I made the plane in time.

I was driving to the airport on a two-lane highway and, realizing the lateness of the hour, put my foot down hard on the gas. In front of me was what must have been another man of the world, because he too was whipping along equally fast. He suddenly swerved out to overtake two cars that were doing barely thirty miles an hour. I had no option but to swerve out also. Just as I got into the left lane the man of the world in front abruptly swung his car back into the right lane, tucking himself into the very small space between the two slow-moving cars. And in front of me was another car, rushing toward me at about the same speed at which I was rushing toward him, and there didn't seem to be any space for me to get out of its way.

But it was done. I did not move, I was too frightened.

When it was over my heart was pounding, my teeth were clenched, and my arms were like water. But at the time somehow, without my doing a thing, all that had been necessary had been done. What was remarkable was that it was done without haste and with great precision. I did not lift a finger to get out of the mess.

Master Ummon once pointed out, "When a man of Ch'an speaks, it is as if he stood unharmed in the midst of flames. He may speak all day but not carry a word in his mouth. He eats and dresses every day, yet it is as if he had neither tasted a grain of rice nor covered himself with so much as a thread."

Shogen Osho came to awakening on hearing his master shout at a monk, "It is not Buddha, it is not mind, it is not a thing!" That is why Mumon states, "It must be said that Shogen shows us all his stomach and intestines. But alas, no one can appreciate him! And even if someone can appreciate him, let him come to me, and I'll beat him severely." Wherever would you find Shogen to appreciate him?

It is of no use, Mumon is saying, trying to understand this koan, understanding is not enough. On the contrary, one must pass through the fire again and again. Shibayama in his commentaries on the *Mumonkan* says, "The koan throws a student into a steep and rugged maze where he has no sense of direction at all. He is expected to overcome all the difficulties and find the way out himself." In other words, the koan is the most difficult and rough passage for the student to go through. Throw it all on the fire, says Mumon. If it burns it is not gold. If it is gold it will not burn.

21 Ummon's Shit Stick

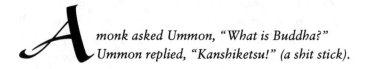

monk asked Ummon, "What is Buddha?"
Ummon replied, "Kanshiketsu!" (a shit stick).

Mumon's Comment

Ummon was too poor to prepare plain food, too busy to speak from notes. He hurriedly took up the shit stick to support the way. The decline of Buddhism was thus foreshadowed.

Mumon's Verse

> Lightning flashing,
> Sparks shooting;
> A moment's blinking,
> "Missed forever."

Comment

The question what is Buddha? does not mean very much to most Westerners. But it must be remembered that in the East the word Buddha was loaded. The question was equivalent to what is God? or what is of ultimate meaning in our lives?

In connection with this koan one cannot help conjuring up the following scene. A prissy monk, full of idealized ideas about Buddha and Buddhism, comes gushing to Ummon asking, "What *is* Buddha?" and Ummon, hardly able to contain his irritation exclaims, "Dried shit!"

But, on reflection we recognize this will not do. It is too insulting, and furthermore it does not have the bite necessary for a koan. Such a reply would be simply to bring Buddha down to the level of dried shit and, apart from anything else, that would be blasphemous.

A dialogue between a Sufi master and his disciple is on record that could be seen as a comment on this koan. The disciple asked the master, "Supposing we see refuse or carrion [or, we could say, a piece of dried shit], will you say that it is God?" The master replied, "God, in his exaltation, forbid that he should be such a thing! Our discourse is with him who doth not see refuse to be refuse or carrion to be carrion; our discourse is with him who hath insight and is not altogether blind."

This koan of Ummon's was a favorite of Ta Hui, a well-known Zen master of eleventh-century China. He used the words dried shit rather than shit stick, and this would probably have more meaning for us. A shit stick was used by the Chinese in lieu of toilet paper. Ta Hui exhorted his followers to use the response dried shit somewhat as one uses mu, bringing all one's concentrative powers to bear on it. He said on one occasion, "Just bring up this saying, 'dried shit!' When all your machinations suddenly come to an end, then you'll awaken. Don't try to get realization from the words or try in your confusion to assess and explain."

Mumon's commentary emphasizes the importance of the spontaneity of Ummon. Ummon's poverty was his great asset, and because of it he was well known for his single-word responses. For example, someone asked him, "What is Buddha?" and he replied, "Grits!" Another time he flung his arms out and said "barrier," indicating that the whole world is a barrier. It is only out of extreme poverty that such clarity can come. It is only out of a mind completely involved in the moment, too busy, as Mumon would say, that the truth of dried shit could have exploded. We are so proud of our opinions about religion, politics, and current affairs, opinions we think of as a mark of a rich personality, that we have to make judgments, we have to establish orders and classes, ranks, and levels. Sweep it all aside in one moment and then, "What is dried shit?" Someone said, "God is so omnipresent that God is an angel in an angel, a stone in a stone, and a straw in a straw."

Unfortunately, all this has complicated the issue terribly, which is a shame because the essence of this koan is simplicity, utter simplicity. Ta Hui exhorts us to take our confused and unhappy minds and shift them onto dried shit! Once we succeed in doing this, the mind that is afraid of death, that is upset and depressed, that has to get it all sorted out, that is so clever, will no longer operate. "As the days and months come and go, of itself your potential will be purified." Then one day

> *Lightning flashing,*
> *Sparks shooting;*
> *Without a moment's blinking*
> *It will reveal itself!*

> *Dried shit.*

22 Ananda and the Flagpole

Ananda asked Kashyapa, "The World-Honored One transmitted to you the robe and bowl; did he transmit anything else to you?" Kashyapa called him and said, "Ananda!" "Yes?" "Knock down the flagpole at the gate."

Mumon's Comment
If you can give a turning word with regard to this, you will see the meeting at Vulture Peak still in session. If not, then this is what Vipasyin Buddha worried about from remote ages; up to now he has still not grasped the essence.

Mumon's Verse

> The question—how dull! The answer—how intimate!
> How many people there are with a film over their
>   eyes!

> *Elder brother calling, younger brother answering—the*
> *family skeleton!*
> *This is a spring that does not belong to Yin and Yang.*

Comment

You may remember the account of the meeting at Vulture
Peak in koan 6. This meeting, Mumon says, is still in
progress. Buddha held up a flower in lieu of giving a talk,
and when he did this no one quite knew what to do except
Mahakashyapa. He smiled. Because of this Buddha transmitted the dharma to him saying, "I have the all pervading
true dharma eye, the marvelous mind of Nirvana, exquisite
teaching of formless form, the subtle dharma gate. It does
not rely on letters and is transmitted outside the scriptures. I
now hand it on to Maha Kasho."

Ananda, who was possibly a nephew of Buddha, was
his personal attendant for many years. It seems he had a
remarkable memory because, so it is said, he was responsible for recording the sutras of Buddha. Nevertheless,
although he was close to the Buddha for about twenty-five
years, he did not come to awakening in Buddha's lifetime.
This koan records his eventual awakening.

His question to Mahakashyapa is a question a lot of
people ask. What is transmission, what did Buddha hand on
to Mahakashyapa? We have to understand transmission on
the one hand as the most simple of all simple issues, and on
the other as something fairly complex. The reason for the
complexity is that Zen finds its place in a very imperfect
world.

We hear about awakening and try to imagine what it
must be like. Failing in this, we come to appreciate that our

discriminating mind, which we rely on to steer us through the maze of life, is unable to grasp the implication of awakening. Thus we are at the mercy, to some extent, of someone who is awakened and whom we need to help us in our blindness. This gives the person power over us. This is unfortunate because, in the words of the British peer Lord Acton, "Power tends to corrupt and absolute power corrupts absolutely."

Transmission is therefore a two-way street. Receiving it, the person is sanctioned to teach; giving it, the person passes on authority. The person who is teaching looks upstream and claims transmission from his teacher, who in turn was empowered by his teacher, and so on up the line. In Zen the patriarchal line purports to trace transmission all the way back to Shakyamuni Buddha and back farther still through the seven legendary Buddhas of whom Vipasyin Buddha is the first.

A similar patriarchal line exists in the Catholic Church. At one time the lineage in the transmission of the power of the pope became confused because the papal seat was moved to Avignon in France. The pope always traced his lineage back to Peter, who in turn, it is claimed, was empowered by Christ. To clear up the confusion, the pope of the time had the papal crown paraded around the streets on a severed head that he claimed was the head of Peter. At the end of the parade the crown was taken off the other head and placed on his own.

The diplomas and certificates adorning the walls of doctors, lawyers, architects, and so on are the modern equivalent of the robe and bowl. They are issued as a way of preventing charlatans from corrupting the professions, and so preserve the trust of the people being served. In the case, say, of doctors, it is fairly obvious what is transmitted to them. A curriculum exists that has to be completed, as well as ways by which to ensure that someone has indeed fulfilled the requirements of this curriculum. A certificate indicates these requirements have been met. But what has been transmitted to Mahakashyapa and his descendants?

The spiritual is its own dimension, and no criteria at the secular level are adequate to judge it. A person asked Nisargadatta whether he should not examine a teacher before he put himself entirely in his hands. Nisargadatta replied, "By all means examine! But what can you find out? Only as he appears to you on your own level." The questioner went on to say that he would watch to ensure that the teacher was consistent, whether harmony existed between his teaching and his life. Nisargadatta argued, "You may find plenty of disharmony—so what? It proves nothing. Only motives matter. How will you know his motives?" The questioner maintained, "I should at least expect him to be a man of self-control who leads a righteous life." Nisargadatta replied, "Such you will find and many, and of no use to you. A teacher can show the way back home, to your real self. What has this to do with the character or the temperament of the person he appears to be? Does he not clearly tell you that he is not the person?"

This in a way is the crux of the issue. This is what the koan is about. If you want to find the way back home you must find a guide who has already made the journey. What is the good of a guide who is urging you to climb the highest peak, who exhorts you not to be afraid of the dark shadows swirling around, who asks you to use your last ounce of energy, if that person has not had the same experience? Transmission should be proof that the successor has made the journey and is competent to help others. Unfortunately, transmission does not always do this. Although the awakening is a basic requirement for teachers, and it is only competent teachers who can certify that this awakening is genuine, nevertheless they should be avoided if they blatantly betray the trust of their students or deliberately use their power to humiliate them.

Someone said the whole universe is an eye, the all-pervading dharma eye, the eye that never sleeps. The marvelous mind of Nirvana is a mind swept clean of all duality, of all this and that, here and there, awakening and no-awakening. The subtle dharma gate is pure without a speck of dust anywhere. Under these circumstances one naturally does not exploit others, as to do so would be self-exploitation. I cannot hurt or humiliate another without suffering myself.

Bodhidharma spoke of Zen as :

No dependence upon words and letters;
Direct pointing to the heart of the human being;
Seeing into one's own nature;
The attainment of Buddhahood.

Attainment of Buddhahood is, as Mumon observes, a spring that does not fit into the annual cycle of seasons. It does not follow the laws of cause and effect as we know them. It is the family skeleton, a disgrace, because as Mumon also points out, even Vipasyin Buddha, the first in the patriarchal line, has still not grasped the essence. To come to awakening is truly to see that no awakening is possible. But one must truly see it, and this seeing for Mumon is disgraceful.

Ananda asks Kashyapa if the World-Honored One transmitted anything to him besides the robe and bowl. The robe and bowl were symbols of transmission, and Ananda was inquiring what transmission really means. What does it mean, "I give you the all-pervading dharma eye, the marvelous mind of Nirvana, and the subtle dharma gate?"

A governor asked Master Ungo a similar question. "It is said the World-Honored One gave a secret talk of holding up a flower, and Kasho by smiling did not conceal it. What does this mean?" Ungo called out, "O, Governor!" "Yes, Master," replied the governor. "Do you understand?" asked Ungo. When the governor answered, "No, I don't," Ungo told him, "If you do not understand, it shows that the World-Honored One did make the secret talk. If you do understand, it means that Kasho did not conceal it."

Kashyapa also called out, "Ananda!" but whereas the governor missed the point, Ananda shot back, "Yes?" It was like two mirrors reflecting the same light. It was like striking a bell: the striking and the sound are not different. Spontaneity, however, is not a question of fast reaction time. Spontaneous response is always original, it is not reflected off another surface. In Zen it is said, if you are going to walk, then walk, don't wobble!

At the time of this koan, when a teacher gave a talk, a flag was hoisted up the flagpole, and when the talk was ended the flag was taken down. The completeness of the question and response is shown by Mahakashyapa saying, not take down the flag, but *knock* down the flagpole. After this, what use is another talk?

One wonders why it was that, after all the years of Buddha's teaching, both directly and indirectly, Ananda comes to awakening only now with Mahakashyapa's call. One often asks of oneself, "When will I come to awakening?" One can only quote Shakespeare in reply to such a question:

> *If 'tis now, 'tis not to be,*
> *if 'tis to be, 'tis not now.*
> *The ripeness is all!*

23 Hui Neng—Beyond Good and Evil

*T*he sixth patriarch was chased by the monk Myo up to Daiyurei. The patriarch, seeing Myo coming, laid the robe and the bowl on a rock and said to him, "This robe represents the faith; is it to be fought for? I allow you to take it away." Myo tried to lift it, but could not. It was as solid and immovable as a mountain. Hesitating and trembling, he ventured, "I came for the teaching, not for the robe. I beg you to teach your servant." The patriarch said, "Don't think 'This is good, that is bad!' At such a moment where is your original face?" At this Myo, all at once, was greatly awakened; his whole body was covered with sweat. With tears streaming down, he bowed and asked, "Beside the secret words and the secret meaning, is there anything else deeper still?" The patriarch answered, "You have realized your true self, and anything deeper comes from your mind alone." Myo observed, "When I was with Obai together with the other monks, I did not awaken to my true *self. Now I have received your instructions it is like a man drinking water for himself, and knowing whether it is cold or warm. You are my teacher!" The patriarch said, "We both have Obai for our teacher. Hold fast to what you have learned from him."*

Mumon's Comment

The sixth patriarch would say this is a state of emergency, needing grandmotherly kindness. It is as though he peeled a fresh litchi, removed the stone, and then put it into your mouth for you. All you have to do is gulp it down.

Mumon's Verse

> *You describe it in vain, you picture it to no avail;*
> *Praising it is useless; stop trying to grasp it!*
> *There is nowhere to hide it;*
> *When the universe is destroyed, it is not destroyed.*

Comment

This is a much longer koan than usual and it has elements that sometimes make it more of a story than a koan. Its essence is to be found in the challenge of the sixth patriarch, "Don't think 'This is good, that is bad!' At such a moment where is your original face?"

Before going on to deal with this let us talk a little about Hui Neng himself and also about this particular incident. Hui Neng is one of the great names in Zen literature. Unfortunately, according to Yampolsky, the translator of Hui Neng's autobiography, all we know for sure about him is that a man by that name lived about that time. Be that as it may, the *Platform Sutra,* which purports to be his autobiography, is a book of great wisdom and compassion.

This is one of two sutras in the collection of sacred writings of Zen Buddhism devoted to a layman's teaching rather than the Buddha's. Its central teaching is in the form of a contest between Hui Neng and the head monk of the monastery. The fifth patriarch wanted to name a successor, so he called on the community to write a gatha, or short poem, showing the depth of their wisdom. All of the monks declined to write a gatha as they were convinced the head monk would be the one chosen. The head monk wrote the following:

> *The body is a bodhi tree,*
> *The mind a mirror bright;*
> *Wipe it carefully day by day*
> *And let no dust alight.*

Hui Neng read this and realized the one who had written it had not seen into the truth. Therefore he wrote:

> *In Bodhi there is no tree,*
> *Nor is there a mirror bright;*
> *In reality there is no thing,*
> *Where can the dust alight?*

It was his uncompromising sense of unity, or wholeness, that compelled him to write these lines. As long as a mirror, *something,* however subtle, is there, duality arises; from duality arises good and bad and so on into the morass of existence. However, this no-mirror must not be construed simply as a blank. For example, on another occasion Hui Neng heard of a master, Wo-Lun, who wrote the following:

> *Wo-Lun has a special skill:*
> *To cut off all thoughts.*

No situation stirs his mind.
The Bodhi tree grows daily within him.

In reply Hui Neng wrote:

Hui-Neng has no special skill,
He cuts off no thoughts.
His mind responds to all situations.
Where can the Bodhi tree grow?

The background to the sutra is as follows. Hui Neng, originally an illiterate peddler of wood, one day heard a monk reciting the *Diamond Sutra*. When the monk came to the line, "Arouse the mind without resting it upon anything," Hui Neng immediately came to great awakening. After this he made arrangements for the care of his aged mother, and left for the monastery from which the monk had come. When he arrived, although a layman, he was nevertheless accepted by the fifth patriarch who recognized his innate capacity. After the incident with the two gathas, the fifth patriarch passed on the patriarchate, symbolized by the robe and bowl, to Hui Neng. But because Hui Neng was young, illiterate, a newcomer, and a layman, the fifth patriarch knew this could well bring down the wrath of the community who would certainly be intensely envious of the man's good fortune. He therefore smuggled Hui Neng out of the monastery at night and advised him to go away, lead the life of a layman for a number of years, and only then begin his life as the sixth patriarch. Hui Neng accepted this counsel and had traveled some considerable way from the monastery when Myo overtook him.

When I first heard this koan I was filled with dismay. My vision of a monastery at the time was an idealistic one in which I imagined all the monks selflessly devoting themselves to spiritual practice, having none of the baser emotions of greed, jealousy, anger, and lust that flourished lavishly in my own psychological back yard. The idea that a monk would chase another monk for what must have been miles because of envy disguised as altruism I found extremely hard to accept.

But as my own Zen training progressed, I discovered that far from resolving the emotion of envy, spiritual practice can sometimes inflame it. Ramana Maharshi tells of the hermit who was so jealous of Maharshi's spirituality that he rolled a huge rock down on him hoping to kill him. Devadatta, Buddha's cousin, made three attempts to kill Buddha. The third patriarch was killed by an enraged Taoist. For the West the prime example of spiritual envy and the havoc it can wreak is the story of the betrayal of Jesus by Judas.

At the center where I did my training, those who passed their first koan were at one time distinguished by being issued a *raksu,* a square ritual robe worn by Buddhist monks. When I first arrived in Montreal a good part of my time was spent counseling people who were consumed with envy because so-and-so had a raksu and they did not. Later the practice of awarding raksus for passing the breakthrough koan was abandoned, and instead the robes were issued to people who had attended a ceremony for taking the ten precepts.

Envy is a mixture of I must have and I can't have. Hidden inside us all is the need to be unique, to be the only one. This paradoxically arises because we *are* the only one. Buddha said when he came to awakening: "Throughout heaven and earth I *alone* am the honored one." He spoke for all of us. Each of us is Buddha; each of us is the honored one. Our problem is that we feel others must know about our uniqueness too. A great part of our effort in life is directed toward seducing others, cajoling them, forcing them, persuading them to accept this. But it has the effect of tearing us apart because the very presence of others proves our claim is mistaken. The more we try, the more glaring the mistake becomes. This is why Sartre was both right and wrong when he said, "*L'enfer, c'est les autres!*" (Hell is other people).

> *In Bodhi there is no tree,*
> *Nor is there a mirror bright;*
> *In reality there is no thing,*
> *Where can the dust alight?*

What Hui Neng was showing when he wrote this gatha was the truth of Buddha's statement, "Throughout Heaven and Earth I alone am the honored one." To arouse the mind without resting it on anything is to declare this truth beyond words. When we allow the mind to dwell on things and thoughts, above all when we allow the mind to dwell on the idea "I am something," we fall into dualism, into thoughts of me and you, good and bad.

The difference between I am and I am something seems so slight that it is scarcely worth taking into account. Yet it is just that tenth of an inch of which Zen speaks that makes all the difference in the world. Egoism is expressed fully in Hitler's "I am, none else beside me," which is the inverse of Buddha's declaration. "None else beside me" means that I will hate those who presume to be beside me. Have you ever noticed that stamp collectors tend to hate other stamp collectors, golf players other golf players, politicians other politicians? We carve out a niche for ourselves and in this niche proclaim, "I am, none else beside me." When others prove us wrong, when others have a bigger stamp collection than ours, have a lower golf handicap, have more power, we hate them, hatred being the wall by which we try to exclude them from our lives.

I remember clearly the day when I realized my aim in life was to be unique. I was talking with a friend, and, as one sometimes does on such occasions, we were discussing another friend. She said, indignantly, "Do you know I actually believe she thinks she is superior to me." For a moment our eyes met. Like a flash the thought rushed through my mind, "And she [the one talking to me] thinks she is superior to me!" Also I knew she was thinking, "And he thinks he is superior to me too!" And I did! Or rather it was so self-evident to me that I was superior I did not even have to think it. I felt terribly embarrassed and did not know what to do. The conversation petered out.

Many people take up Zen in the hope that at last they will have found the way by which they can discover to their own and others' satisfaction that they are special. The dream of the misunderstood child who becomes a princess overnight, a Cinderella, or a hero, seems at last capable of being fulfilled. On this side of the gateless gate one can only dream and imagine what it must be like to penetrate, to know one's own true nature. When others break through it is in a way a fundamental betrayal. Not only has someone else won the prize, but the prize has lost its earlier value of being able to confer uniqueness upon me. I am doubly denied. The pain from this can be excruciating. It was the pain that drove Myo to run after Hui Neng.

Before he became a monk Myo was a general, and he

must have been into middle age by the time of this koan. The fact he was a monk probably means he had suffered a great change in his life, one very likely brought about by some deep betrayal. The decision to give up the authority and power of a general for the life of obscurity and anonymity of a monk must have been backed by pain that no doubt would have fueled his practice. The general would have felt great loyalty to his teacher who, more than likely, was the head monk whom everyone expected to become the new patriarch. Through the head monk Myo thought he could realize his great dream. And now this uncouth youth, with no long training to back him up, with no understanding of the sutras or what Buddhism really meant, had in some way duped the fifth patriarch and persuaded him to give him the patriarchate! Driven by pain channeled into loyalty and idealism he was determined to show the thief what was right, and so enable good to triumph over evil, right to vanquish wrong. Drawn by this vision of the ideal, driven by pain, he rushed along after the sixth patriarch. When the general caught up with him, instead of resisting him, instead of putting up a fight, or even trying to argue with him, Hui Neng just put down the coveted robe and bowl and said, "This robe represents the faith; is it to be fought for? I allow you to take it away."

But Myo could not move the robe and bowl, try how he may. My teacher Roshi Kapleau always insisted we should not interpret this psychologically. This was a moment of great doubt for the general. Anyone who has practiced for a long time trying to resolve the koan of life knows this moment when one's force is no longer of any avail. One is like Hakuin's rat in a bamboo tube. One is caught up in one's own contradiction.

The opposite state is described by Jesus in the Gospel of St. Thomas: "If two make peace with one another in the same house, they will say to the mountain, Move! and it will move."

All the general could do was pant that he wanted to learn, not take the robe. But Hui Neng instead inquired after Myo's original self, the self he knew is the no-self that is undivided without inside or outside, that is the world and yet beyond the world, that sustains all without itself having any support.

Myo's sweat and tears were from sheer relief. Yet his awakening was not complete because he still had to know if there was "anything deeper." The patriarch told him, "You have realized your true self, anything deeper belongs to you alone."

The whole spirit of this koan is summed up so well by Mumon's verse:

You describe it in vain, you picture it to no avail;
Praising it is useless; stop trying to grasp it!
There is nowhere to hide it;
When the universe is destroyed, it is not destroyed.

Beyond something and nothing, what is it?

24 Fuketsu—Beyond Speech and Silence

A monk asked Fuketsu, "Both speech and silence transgress; how can we avoid this transgression?" Fuketsu said, "I often think of Konan in March; The partridge chirps among the scented flowers."

Mumon's Comment

Fuketsu's Zen is like lightning. He has his road and walks along it. But why does he not avoid relying on the tongues of the ancients? If you really grasp the problem, you know there is a way out; leave all words and phrases behind and say something.

Mumon's Verse

> *He did not use a refined phrase;*
> *Before speaking he had already made the point.*
> *If Fuketsu had gone on talking and chattering,*
> *The monk would not have got "it."*

Comment

Koans are not hurdles to be jumped over. Their practice is more like appreciation. They are objective works of art, to borrow a term from Gurdjieff, and just like any work of art of merit, they require sustained attention and appreciation. Once one sees this one realizes that koans are small jewels to be treated with great care, and one never tires of them. They are not like a riddle that once solved loses its interest, but like great music: the more one can appreciate what cannot be explained, the richer it becomes.

One can listen to a sonata and say, "That is wonderful." After listening to it a few more times one says, "I really appreciate that now." After a few more times one wonders how one could have ever said after just hearing it once that one had enjoyed it, so much richer now is one's appreciation. Each hearing brings a new richness. But you would be hard put to reply if someone were to challenge you and ask, "What do you mean, 'richer'?"

This koan reminds one of the conversation that Sariputra had with a goddess who, for the occasion, had transformed herself into a woman (we referred to this conversation earlier). The goddess said, "All words that you speak are of themselves awakening. Why? Because awakening is in all things." "But is not awakening to be free from greed, anger, and ignorance?" asked Sariputra. The goddess replied, "To say that awakening is freedom from greed, anger, and ignorance is the teaching for the excessively proud. Those free of pride are taught that the very nature of greed, anger, and ignorance is itself awakening."

Here we see the essence of the *Prajnaparamita* Way: "Nirvana is samsara, samsara is Nirvana."

Fuketsu—Beyond Speech and Silence

The questioner in the koan must have been well versed in the truth to be able to ask his question. It is not uncommon for us to believe that in silence is wisdom. We are reminded of Lao Tzu's "The one who speaks does not know, the one who knows does not speak." A famous Hindu teacher spent a large part of his life in silence and was considered a wise man as a consequence. However, the questioner says that both forms, whether of speech or silence, cannot contain the truth. They both transgress, or are both too much. How can we avoid this transgression?

Fuketsu said, "I often think of Konan in March; / The partridge chirps among the scented flowers." These were words of an ancient Chinese poet, and we can be sure they must have had a special place in Fuketsu's heart. But where was Fuketsu when he answered in this way? If you can answer this question you will have answered Mumon's question, "But why does Fuketsu not avoid relying on the tongues of the ancients?"

25 Kyozan's Dream

*W*hile dreaming, Kyozan went to Maitreya's
place and was asked to sit in the third seat.
*A senior monk struck the table with a gavel and announced,
"Today the one in the third seat is due to speak." Kyozan
rose and, striking the table with the gavel, stated, "The truth
of Mahayana is beyond the four propositions and the hundred negations. Listen! Listen!"*

Mumon's Comment
Now tell me, did Kyozan give a teisho or not? If you open
your mouth you are lost; if you do not open your mouth,
you are lost. Even if you neither open nor close your mouth,
you are a hundred and eight thousand miles away from the
truth.

Mumon's Verse

Broad daylight under a bright blue sky;
He speaks of a dream in a dream;
Watch out!
He's trying to deceive you all.

Comment

Kyozan had a very close relationship with his teacher Isan, out of which a number of stories have come. One is similar to a mondo we gave earlier. One day when they were picking tea, Isan called to Kyozan, "All day I have heard your voice but have not seen your face." Kyozan, not saying anything, shook a tea plant. Isan said, "You have got the function but not the essence." "So, what would you say?" asked Kyozan. Isan remained silent. Then Kyozan told him, "You have the essence but not the function."

During another mondo Isan asked Kyozan, "In the forty volumes of the *Nirvana Sutra*, how many words were spoken by Buddha and how many by the devils?" Kyozan replied, "They are all devils' words." Isan said, "From now on no one will be able to do anything to you."

On another occasion when Isan was in bed Kyozan came to speak to him, but the master turned his face to the wall. Kyozan asked, "How can you do this?" The master rose and stated, "A moment ago I had a dream. Won't you interpret it for me?" Thereupon Kyozan brought in a basin of water for the master to wash his face. A little later Hsiang-yen also appeared to speak to the master. The master repeated, "I have just had a dream. Yang-shan [Kyozan] interpreted it. Now it is your turn." Hsiang-yen brought in a cup of tea. The master said, "The insight of both of you excels that of Sariputra."

It is often said the world is a dream, and so many people mistakenly believe awakening is to awaken to an entirely new world, one that is somehow transcendent. This puzzles them because they wonder what kind of world it could be. Some believe some special skill or attribute, even a capacity to perform miracles, comes with awakening. Layman P'ang in a verse after his awakening said, "This special power to perform magic and miracles is in drawing water and chopping wood." We do not wake up *from* a dream, but rather we wake up *to* the dream. Some, hearing that the world is a dream, assent to it intellectually but at the same time secretly think of it as a poetic way of talking. They believe the dream is real, and this is the deepest dream of all.

One of the lines chanted at the Montreal Zen Center is, "May the power of your samadhi sustain us." This is the power of the samadhi of Buddhas and patriarchs. However, the power of our own samadhi in turn sustains Buddhas and patriarchs, and also the whole world and all that is in it. To wake up to the dream is to see the truth of this. It is like a glass of pure water into which a drop of deep blue ink is dropped. The ink swirls and makes patterns. You are the clear pure water, the world is the swirling patterns of the deep blue ink.

One of the most striking features of a dream is that it and the dreamer are one. In a dream we do not have a sense of separation, of me here, the world over there. We see the dream in the same way we see a reflection in a mirror; whereas we are constantly aware that the mirror is there, we are not directly aware *of* the mirror itself. So it is in a dream, although now the mirror is awareness itself. When we wake up into everyday awareness we say the dream fades. By this we mean the sense of wholeness implicit in a dream gives way to the usual, dichotomous view of the world. This we say is the real world. But this too is a dream, although this time the dream is the dream that the dream is real.

Isan sent Kyogen a mirror, and during a teisho Kyogen asked, "Is this Isan's mirror or mine? If you say it is mine, did it not come from Isan? If you say it is Isan's, am I not now holding it? If you can say a word of Zen I will keep the mirror, if not I will break it." Putting the question slightly differently we could ask, who owns awareness?

When the monk says, "the truth of Mahayana is beyond the four propositions and the hundred negations," does he mean that the Mahayana is beyond the dichotomous view of the world? The four propositions are the world is separate from me, the world is not separate from me, the world both is and is not separate from me, and the world neither is nor is not separate from me. The hundred negations are permutations of these four in their various forms. In other words, is the Mahayana truth beyond the real world as we know it?

The third seat in a monastery is given over to the "timer," the person who uses the instruments to begin and end a period of sitting. At the Montreal Zen Center these instruments are a pair of clappers and a bell. When the clappers are struck, they make a very sharp crack. This is by way of calling people back from their dreams into the moment.

The koan revolves around the senior monk's announcement, "Today the one in the third seat is due to speak." On another occasion the head monk complained to Kyozan that he had not given any teisho: Kyozan ordered the han and gong to be struck to announce a teisho, and the assembly gathered. Kyozan ascended the rostrum, and after sitting there for a while, he descended and returned to his room. The head monk followed him and complained, "You agreed to give a teisho. How is it that you uttered not a word?" Kyozan explained, "For sutras there are sutra specialists. For sastras there are sastra specialists. Why do you wonder at this old monk's behavior?"

Before an assembly of Buddhas, what kind of talk would you give?

The old pond,
The frog jumps in,
Plop!
—Basho

26 Two Monks Roll Up the Blinds

When the monks assembled before the midday meal to listen to his teisho, Hogen pointed to the bamboo blinds. Two monks simultaneously rolled them up in an identical way. Hogen said, "One has it, the other doesn't."

Mumon's Comment
Tell me, who had it and who didn't? If your eye is open on this point, you will see where Hogen failed. However, I warn you strongly against discriminating between has and has not.

Mumon's Verse

When the blinds are rolled up, the great sky is bright
   clear and empty,
But the great empty sky is not the way of Zen.

> *Throw away the empty sky,*
> *Just let the breeze waft through.*

Comment

Someone asked Hogen, "What is Buddha?" Hogen replied, "First I want you to practice it, second I want you to practice it."

Just as it is useful to know that Tokusan was an exponent of the *Diamond Sutra* before he became a Zen monk, and that Joshu was fond of quoting from the third patriarch's *Verses on the Faith Mind,* so it is useful to know that before he became a Zen master Hogen was an exponent of the *Hwa Yen.* This sutra was very popular in China and probably many Zen monks studied it in depth. A demonstration of its principles was given by Fa Tsang, an exponent of the *Hwa Yen.* A brief summary of this is given in Appendix 4, and it might be of interest to read this extract before going ahead, as the koan has close connections with it.

One of the more enigmatic mondo has a monk asking Master Hogen, "What is a drop of water from the source of So?" Hogen replies, "A drop of water from the source of So." "So" refers to Sokei, the name given to the sixth patriarch. The question is asking what is the essence of Sokei's teaching? It is evident that a drop of water from the source of So remains that no matter whether it is clean or dirty, whether it is a big drop or a small drop, whether it is warm or cold. Similarly, sometimes it is not so important what we say as that we say it. Seen from this point of view, to say one thing is to say everything. This same theme runs through a mondo involving P'ang, a famous lay Buddhist of the eighth century. P'ang asked Baso, "Who is the man who doesn't accompany the ten thousand dharmas?" Baso replied, "Wait till you have swallowed all the water of the West river in one gulp and I will tell you."

One of the biggest hindrances to seeing into this mondo and the koan is the firm conviction one is something in a world of somethings. That one is, moreover, a part of some great whole. However, no parts can ever be found, everything is the whole.

On the face of it, this is a repetition of koan 11 about Joshu and the two hermits. In both koans two people do identical things: in the first, one is praised and the other condemned; in the second, one has it and the other doesn't. Nevertheless, they are by no means saying the same thing.

A mondo between Nansen and two monks gives a very similar flavor to that of the present koan. Nansen asked a monk: "Last night there was a nice breeze?" The monk replied: "Last night there was a nice breeze." Nansen: "A branch was blown off the pine in front of the gate?" Monk: "A branch was blown off the pine in front of the gate." Nansen asked another monk: "Last night there was a nice breeze?" Monk: "What breeze?" Nansen: "A branch was blown off the pine in front of the gate?" Monk: "What branch?" Nansen concluded, "One has it, the other doesn't."

One is tempted to think that it is the first who has it and the second who doesn't, but one would miss the point of the mondo to think this. It is said that emptiness is form and form is emptiness. Does emptiness have it, or does form?

Mumon warns strongly against discriminating between has and has not. But did not Hogen make a discrimination? Or did he? Is this what Mumon means when he says Hogen failed, that he failed to make a discrimination? In which case the failure would be glorious. Someone said everything is unique, there is no difference, so how can things be compared?

27 The Truth that No One Has Taught

A monk asked Nansen, "Is there a truth which no one has yet taught?" Nansen replied, "There is." "What is this truth which no one so far has taught?" asked the monk. Nansen answered, "It is not mind, not Buddha, not things."

Mumon's Comment

Nansen, being asked one question, spends all his wealth at once. What a fraud!

Mumon's Verse

> Say too much and you lose your worth;
> No-words have great power!
> Even in a blue moon
> You can never be told it.

Comment

This same koan is given in the *Hekiganroku* (case 28) but with some slight differences. Hyakujo asks the question, and then, after Nansen has replied as above, asks the further question probably most of us would want to ask, "Aren't you teaching it now?" Nansen then says, "Yes, I am. What about you?" Hyakujo says, "I am not a great master. How can I know whether there is preaching or non-preaching?" Nansen says, "I don't understand." Hyakujo says, "I have taught it thoroughly."

Negation has been a way by which mystics have attempted to express transcendental unity. In the Christian tradition, for example, there are two streams: the kataphatic and the apophatic, the affirmative and the negative. Thomas Merton, the Trappist monk who did much to revive the contemplative tradition of Christianity, said the kataphatic is "the tradition of light; it arrives at an understanding of God through affirmation: we come to know God by affirming he possesses all the perfection we find in creatures." But, he says, this tradition cannot penetrate to the deepest essence. The apophatic tradition "concerns itself with the most fundamental datum of all faith—and one that is often forgotten: the God who reveals Himself to us in His Word has revealed himself as *unknown* in his ultimate essence. The presence of God is 'known' not in clear vision, but as 'unknown.'"

God, as referred to here, is a God of extreme subtlety. God is, but is unknown. His being is absolute, but absolutely unknowable. Absolute transcendental unity is affirmed, but as unknowable. On the face of it it would seem this koan, as well as other similar ones, is in the apophatic tradition. Truth *is,* but is inexpressible because unknowable.

However, it is just this fundamental error that the koan is tackling. The problem with the apophatic tradition, or *via negativa* as it is more widely known, is that God still *is*. In other words, God is still the Supreme *Being*. It is something like the gatha of the head monk in the koan about Hui Neng:

> *The body is a bodhi tree,*
> *The mind a mirror bright;*
> *Wipe it carefully day by day*
> *And let no dust alight.*

The clean mirror without dust is pure being, the supreme being, and being pure without qualities, is unknowable. Hui Neng says one must go beyond the mirror, beyond the last vestige of being or not-being.

Hyakujo and Nansen were brother monks and probably evenly matched. They were both deeply awakened, and the *Hekiganroku* version of the koan is undoubtedly a dharma duel, which, one might say, ended in a draw.

Hyakujo asked, "What is the teaching that no one has taught?" This is a very clever question. How can Nansen reply? He goes ahead and teaches: "It is not mind, not Buddha, not things." Naturally Hyakujo says, "But aren't you, by saying that, already teaching what no one can be taught? Who are you that can do what no one else can do!?" And Nansen states, "Yes, I am teaching. That is how I am." A monk asked another monk whether he agreed with all that his teacher had said. The monk replied, "I accept fifty percent, but fifty percent I cannot accept." "Why not?" asked the other monk. "Because I would not be true to my teacher if I accepted it one hundred percent." It is this other fifty percent that the monk cannot accept that Nansen is teaching. It could be said he is teaching that emptiness is form. But the real question is, how is he teaching it?

In connection with this koan of Nansen's, some one asks of Joshu, "It is said that true teaching has no form. But when there is no master and no pupil, how is it then?" Joshu said, "Who made you come to ask this question?" "No one in particular," replied the monk. At that Joshu hit him.

On another occasion a monk asked Joshu, "What is the realm in which there is neither day nor night?" This after all is the realm about which no one has taught anything. Joshu replied, "Is it day now? Is it night now?" The questioner retorted, "I am not asking about now." Joshu retorted, "You cannot do away with me."

Nansen asked Hyakujo, "What about you?" Hyakujo replied, "I am not a great master. How can I know whether there is preaching or nonpreaching?" Was Hyakujo simply being modest? It could be said he was teaching form is emptiness.

A monk once asked a master, "What is the truth that all Buddhas and masters have taught?" The master told him, "Ask the wall." The monk replied, "I do not understand." The master went on to say, "I do not understand either." The monk and the master both say "I do not understand," but are they saying the same thing?

28 Ryutan Blows Out the Candle

Tokusan and Ryutan spent all night discussing Zen. At last Ryutan said, "It is late. Time for you to go." Tokusan thanked him and departed, but outside the temple he found it was very dark, so he went back in. Ryutan lit a candle and handed it to him, and the moment that Tokusan took it, whoo! Ryutan blew it out. At this, immediately, Tokusan came to awakening.

Ryutan asked, "What have you seen?" Tokusan said, "From now on I know that the ancients did not lie."

The next day Ryutan ascended the rostrum and said, "There is one among you whose fangs are like swords and whose mouth is a bowl of blood. Strike him with a stick but he will not turn his head. Some day he will climb the highest peak to establish our way there."

Tokusan took his notes on the Diamond Sutra *to the front of the temple and, with a flaming torch in his hand, said, "Even though you have conquered the esoteric doctrines, it is like throwing a hair into vast space. Even though you have learned all the secrets of the world, it is like a drop of water dripping into the vast ocean." And he set light to all his notes. Then, making a bow, he took leave of his teacher.*

Mumon's Comment

Before Tokusan crossed the barrier from his native place, his mind burned with resentment and his mouth was bitter. He went south to stamp out the doctrine of the special transmission outside the sutras. When he reached the road to Reishu, he asked an old woman to let him have some tea and cookies (literally in Chinese, *mind refreshers*). "Your honor, what sort of books are you carrying in your bag?" the old woman asked. "Commentaries on the *Diamond Sutra*," replied Tokusan. The old woman said, "I hear it is said in the sutra, 'It is impossible to retain past mind, impossible to hold on to present mind and impossible to grasp future mind.' Now I would ask you, what mind are you going to refresh?" Tokusan was dumbfounded. He then asked, "Do you know of any good teachers around here?" The old woman said, "Five miles down the road you will find Ryutan Osho."

Coming to Ryutan, things just got worse for Tokusan. His former words did not match his later ones. As for Ryutan, he seemed to have lost all sense of shame in his compassion toward his son. Finding a bit of live coal in the other, enough to start a fire, he hurriedly poured muddy water to put it out at once. A little cool reflection tells us it was all a farce.

Mumon's Verse

> *Better to see the face than hear the name.*
> *Better to hear the name than see the face.*

Ryutan Blows Out the Candle

He may have saved his nose
But, alas! he lost his eyes.

Comment

This is the same Tokusan whom we encountered in koan 13, but at the time of this koan he was still young and full of fire, or at least he was full of fire until he met Ryutan. Tokusan lived in the north of China and was an exponent of the *Diamond Sutra*, but he was what we would call a scholar, with only an intellectual understanding of the sutra. When he heard of the Zen sect which said it was possible to attain to Buddhahood within a lifetime, he became incensed and left home to show the southern barbarians the error of their ways. That is what Mumon means by saying, "Before Tokusan crossed the barrier from his native place, his mind burned with resentment and his mouth was bitter. He went south to stamp out the doctrine of the special transmission outside the sutras."

And he met the old woman.

It is true that Buddhism, alas, was no exception to the rule of earlier times in looking on women as inferior to men. However, in the Zen sect it was always insisted that women, no less than men, could see into their true nature. All, without distinction of race, color, or sex, are Buddha. That Zen regarded men and women as equal is brought out in many of the stories of Zen in which women unseat the mighty and deflate the pompous. This koan is an account of such a deflation.

No doubt Tokusan must have been very proud of his knowledge of Buddhism, particularly of the *Diamond Sutra*. He was going to set the world to rights, and in particular he wanted to do battle with the masters who were teaching heretical doctrines. On the way he rests at a tea house. Tired no doubt, hungry and thirsty surely, but nevertheless buoyed in the security of his arrogance, he asks for "mind refreshers," cakes that were as common to the Chinese as doughnuts are to us. Then the old lady quotes the *Diamond Sutra*, the very one in which Tokusan is an expert, "It is impossible to retain past mind, impossible to hold on to present mind and impossible to grasp future mind," and demands to know what mind he is going to refresh. One can only imagine Tokusan's consternation. Here he is, an expert, confronted by an ignorant old lady and he is completely stumped! It must have been a moment of supreme humiliation.

He spent the evening talking with Ryutan about Zen. No doubt he would have recounted the story about the old lady and Ryutan would have fed the flames of his confusion. Then it was time to leave. Tokusan says it is dark, so Ryutan gives him a lighted candle. Just as Tokusan is about to take it, Ryutan blows it out. Tokusan comes to awakening. What did he see?

A lovely old hymn sings,

Lead kindly light amid the encircling gloom,
Lead thou me on.
The night is dark and I am far from home,
Lead thou me on.
Guide thou my feet.
I do not ask to see
The distant scene,
One step enough for me.

But what happens when the light goes out? How dark it would be. In such darkness what could be seen? The alchemists say, "Our sun is a black sun." Someone asked

Joshu, "I have heard that men of old said, 'It is void, it is clear, it shines of itself.' To shine of itself, what does that mean?" Joshu said, "It does not mean that something else shines." The monk was still not satisfied and asked further still, "When it fails to shine, what then?" Joshu retorted, "You have betrayed yourself."

In St. John's Gospel it says, "In him the Word was life and *the life was the light of men.* And the light shines in the darkness and the darkness comprehendeth it not." Life is the light of humankind. Ramana Maharshi throws some light on what is meant when he says, "In order to know anything, illumination is necessary. This can only be of the nature of light. However it lights up both physical light and physical darkness, That is to say, it lies beyond light and darkness." However, with all of this, we must be sure that more than a beautiful metaphor is being used. This is why in the koan a concrete situation is acted out.

Ummon once observed, "There is a difference between seeing the light and being the light. Everyone has his own light. If he tries to see it everything is darkness. What is everyone's light? The kitchen pantry and the main gate. A good thing is not as good as no thing." This is not far from the Gnostic who said, "O holy knowing, by thee am I illumined and through thee do I sing praise to the incorporeal light. . . . I rejoice in joy of mind."

Dogen tells the story of an emperor who, during the dedication ceremony for a pagoda he had had built, saw a brilliant light. All of his entourage congratulated him on his good fortune except one man who was a follower of Buddha's Way. The emperor asked him why he did not praise him as the others had done, and the man replied, "Once I read in the sutras that the light of Buddha was not

red, blue, yellow, white, or any natural color. The light that
you saw was not the light of Buddha, but of the dragon that
protects you." The emperor asked, "Well then, what is the
light of Buddha?" The man was silent. Dogen commented, "People who think they are separated from divine light
also believe that divine light is red, white, blue, or yellow,
similar to the light from a fire, or the reflected light of
water, or the sparkle of gems or jewels, or the light of a
dragon, or like sun and moon lights."

He had earlier quoted master Chosa who said, "The
entire world is reflected by the eye of a monk, the entire
world is contained in every day conversation, the entire
world is throughout your body. The entire world is your
own divine light; the entire world is within your own light.
And the entire world is inseparable from yourself."

A Zen Master said:

> *Right within light there's darkness,*
> *But don't see it as darkness:*
> *Right within darkness there's light,*
> *But don't meet it as light.*

29 Hui Neng's Flag

*T*he wind was flapping a temple flag, and two
monks were arguing about it. One said the flag
moved, the other said the wind moved; they argued back
and forth but could not reach a conclusion. The sixth patriarch said, "It is not the wind that moves, it is not the flag
that moves, it is your honorable mind that moves." The
monks were struck with awe.

Mumon's Comment

It is not the wind that moves; it is not the flag that moves, it
is not the mind that moves. Where do you see the real patriarch? If you can get a real understanding of this you will see
that the two monks, wanting to buy iron, got gold. The
patriarch in his compassion was disgraced.

Mumon's Verse

> Wind, flag, mind moving,
> All miss the point.

Only knowing how to open his mouth,
Unaware of his fault in talking.

Comment

It is said this koan records an incident that occurred just as Hui Neng was about to assume the role of sixth patriarch. After the fifth patriarch had transmitted the robe and bowl to Hui Neng, he advised him to live a lay life for some years until he had gained in maturity. Our ordinary life is the perfect life for the true practice of spirituality. The idea we have to live in a special place doing special things would seem to indicate awakening to one's true nature is in itself something special and out of the run of normal existence. On the contrary, awakening is coming home and requires no special activity. Hui Neng, on one occasion said, "The samadhi of oneness is authentic at all times, walking, standing, sitting, and lying. Authentic mind is the place of practice; authentic mind is the pure land. Good friends, some people teach men to sit observing the mind and observing purity, not moving and not arousing the mind and to this they devote their efforts. Deluded people do not realize this is wrong, cling to this doctrine, and so become confused. There are many such people. Those who instruct in this way are from the outset greatly mistaken."

Unfortunately, many have interpreted this to mean that one should not do zazen. Rather, it means one should not bring a special mind to zazen.

The patriarch of the northern school advocated the specific kind of practice Hui Neng was opposed to: he used to tell his disciples to concentrate their minds on quietness, to sit doing zazen for a long time, and, as far as possible, not to lie down. One of these monks went to the sixth patriarch to ask him about this kind of practice and was told, "To concentrate the mind on quietness is a disease of the mind, and not Zen at all. What an idea! restricting the body to sitting all the time! That is useless." He gave the monk the following verse:

> *To sit and not to lie down during one's lifetime,*
> *To lie and never sit during one's lifetime,*
> *Why should we thus task this old bag of bones?*

The great danger then and now is that people will sit in a dead void, in what the masters called the cave of demons. Hui Neng declared quite specifically that one should not cling to the void, and if one sits in meditation with a vacant mind one will fall into torpid apathy.

The two monks are arguing about the flag, disputing what is cause and what is effect. To argue about a flag might seem strange, but they could have as well been arguing about whether we have free will or are determined. Does the wind, that is, circumstances, move the flag, or is it the flag that moves? Which is cause, which effect? Although most of us do not think about that kind of thing very much, that does not mean the debate has no bearing on our lives. On the contrary, our mind is split at a subliminal level, which forces us constantly into making judgments and assessments, fracturing our world in all kinds of ways. We feel people are always trying to frustrate us, thwart us in what we want to do; the world seems unfair and out of joint, we feel unlucky and mistreated. The more we try to sort it all out, decide what is best, and anticipate the problems before they strike, the worse it seems to be. Are the circumstances the problem or is the problem all of our frantic efforts to set things right?

The sixth patriarch told the monks it was their minds that move. Without the constant need to make assessments and judgments, without the constant need to find what is right, what is good, what is true, we would not become prey to the dichotomies of life. If the mind is at one it will naturally seek the good and the true without reducing them to concepts, dogmas, rules, and commandments. If the mind is at one it will naturally seek harmony with others and peace with the world. This is what underlies the sixth patriarch's statement. But what does he really mean by it? Mumon asks, "Where is the real Hui Neng?" Where was the man's mind when he said, "It is your honorable minds that move"?

The clue, as is so often the case, comes from Mumon's comment. Mumon is actually using the words of a nun who was preparing food for some of Hui Neng's disciples when they were visiting her convent and overheard them discussing this statement of Hui Neng's, wondering what he could have meant. It was she who then said, "It is not the wind that moves, it is not the flag that moves, it is not the mind that moves." On the face of it, it would seem the nun is contradicting, or at the very least going one better than, Hui Neng. However, they are both seeing with the same eye. One could say that which changes never changes, that which moves never moves.

We see red flowers, green leaves, black roads, and gray buildings, but all the time we are seeing light. The light is always light. Or we could say we see red flowers, green leaves, black roads, and gray buildings, but all the time we are seeing mind. Mind is always mind. The mind is immutable. A master put it this way: "The real nature does not decrease in the fool nor increase in the sage; it is unperturbed in the midst of trials, nor does it stay still in the depths of meditation and samadhi; it is neither impermanent not permanent; it neither comes nor goes; it is neither in the middle nor in the interior nor in the exterior; it is not born nor does it die; both its essence and its manifestations are in the absolute state of suchness eternal and unchanging, we call it 'Tao.'"

30 Baso's "This Very Mind Is Buddha"

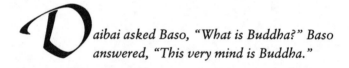

aibai asked Baso, "What is Buddha?" Baso answered, "This very mind is Buddha."

Mumon's Comment

If you have grasped Baso's meaning, you are wearing Buddha's clothes, eating Buddha's food, speaking Buddha's words, doing Buddha's deeds, that is to say, you are Buddha himself. But though this may be so, Daibai has led many a one to confuse the mark on the balance for the weight itself. Didn't he realize that if we explain the word "Buddha" we must rinse out our mouths for the next three days? If he had known this, when he heard Baso say, "The mind is the Buddha," he would have covered his ears and rushed away.

Baso's "This Very Mind is Buddha"

Mumon's Verse

Broad daylight under a bright blue sky,
No more need to search.
"What is Buddha?" you ask;
Even with loot in your pocket, you say you are
*   innocent.*

Comment

A Zen story tells of a young acolyte who after being with his master for three years announced one day he was leaving. "Oh! Why are you leaving?" asked the master. "I have been here three years and you have not taught me a thing." "Really," responded the master. "But when you have brought me tea have I not drunk it?" "Yes." "And when you have bowed, have I not acknowledged it?" "Yes." "And when it is time for bed have I not left for my room?" "Yes," declared the monk for the third time. "Then how can you say I have not taught you?"

What is this very mind? To call it Buddha is to poison it. To call Buddha this very mind is to confuse. It was Joshu who originally said, "When I speak the word Buddha I want to wash my mouth out for three days afterwards." That is how it has become with words such as love, religion, and holiness: they leave a rancid taste in the mouth. Sentimentality, said Oscar Wilde, is to enjoy an emotion for which one has not paid the price; or, one might say, for which one has paid with counterfeit coin.

Baso must have known this, so what did he mean by this very mind? At the moment he said the words, where was the mind? Mumon says, "Broad daylight under a bright blue sky." Baso says, "This very mind." What is the connection?

As another master described, "The hills, fields, sky, and stream, these are my face; the songs of the birds, this is my voice; the wind as it blows through the grass, this is my action." This was echoed in a poignant way by a young Canadian who, during World War II, was a cabin boy living in Copenhagen; he was arrested by the Nazis on the grounds that he was smuggling arms, and was executed at the age of twenty-two. In a letter to his mother he said, "I know you are a courageous woman and you will bear this [news of his pending execution] but, hear me, it is not enough to bear it, you must understand it. I am an insignificant thing, and my person will soon be forgotten, but *the thought, the life, the inspiration that filled me will live on. You will meet them everywhere—in the trees at springtime, in people who cross your path, in a loving little smile*" (my emphasis).[7]

A monk asked Joshu, "Who is the one that transcends even Buddha?" Joshu replied, "That man leading his oxen, it is he." We might say instead, the cabin boy. We might also say, the man who executed him. Even in his ignorance, he too was wearing Buddha's clothes, eating Buddha's food, speaking Buddha's words, doing Buddha's deeds; that is to say, he too was Buddha. Someone asked Yasutani Roshi, "What is the difference between you and me?" Yasutani said, "There is no difference, but I know it." In that knowing is all, it is the gateway, as one master put it, to all mysteries, and we all know it. So, right at this very moment, what is Buddha?

---

[7] From *Dying We Live: Letters Written by Prisoners in Germany on the Verge of Execution.* H. Gollwitzler, K. Kohn, and R. Schneider eds., trans. by R. C. Kuhn. (London: Fontana Books, 1958).

31 Joshu Investigates the Old Woman

A monk asked an old woman, "What is the way to Gutei?" The old woman directed him, "Go straight on." When the monk had walked a few steps, she remarked, "He may be a fine-looking monk, but he is just an ordinary one like the rest."

Later on someone told Joshu about this and Joshu said, "Wait a moment, I will go and see into the old woman for you." The next day he went to the old woman, asked the same question, and was given the same answer.

He said to his disciples, "I have seen into the old woman for you."

Mumon's Comment

The old woman just knew how to sit in her tent and plan the campaign; she did not know she was being infiltrated by a spy. Though old Joshu showed himself clever enough to steal into the camp and take the fortress, he gave no sign of being a great general. If we think about it, they both have their faults. But tell me, what did Joshu see in the old woman?

Mumon's Verse

> *The question was the same,*
> *The answer was the same,*
> *Sand in the rice,*
> *Thorns in the mud.*

Comment

This is the most difficult of all the koans in the *Mumonkan*, but at the same time the most complete. It contains within its simple story the unfolding from the first kensho to full awakening. One has to pay careful attention to all that Mumon says, he does not waste a single word either in his commentary or in his verse, and everything he says must be included in the resolution of the koan.

We are familiar with Joshu and encountered his own kensho in an earlier koan: *everyday mind is the way*. This is an elaboration on that koan.

Once again we have an old woman. This time she wrestles, perhaps unwisely, with Joshu. But even Joshu could not best her because, after all, he must somehow have given himself away. This is a dharma duel, and to penetrate the koan we should see that the woman is deeply awakened.

What does an awakened person look like? In the West in particular we have a romantic view of such a person. In part this is due to our confusion between an awakened person and a saint, whose sanctification depends on miracles. We believe we would be, or should be, in the presence of the miraculous were we in the presence of a saint, and we feel the same should be true of an awakened person. In Zen, however, the miracle is not to walk on water but to walk at all; it is not to speak in tongues, but to speak. Zen is coming down to earth and finding it is heaven.

Another reason for our misunderstanding is that, at some level, we think awakening must be in some way an exaltation of the ego. Wagner's opera *Parsifal* truly exemplifies this. As portrayed by Wagner, spirituality is pure glorification of the known. In the stage directions for the final climax of the opera it is says, "Parsifal mounts the altar steps, takes the Grail from the shrine . . . and falls before it in silent contemplation. The Grail begins to glow with a soft light, with darkness coming in below and increasing light coming from above. Then *a beam of light: the Grail glows at its brightest. From the dome a white dove descends and hovers above Parsifal's head. . . .*" (my italics).

In contrast I remember seeing Yasutani Roshi one day kneeling on the grass of a hunting and fishing camp in Ontario, where he had just finished giving an introductory weekend *zazenkai*, or workshop. His head was almost touching the ground in front of the monk Taisan who was shaving it. Surrounded by rickety old shacks, none of which had a perpendicular wall, this tiny old man in a battered robe knelt in the dust on tough old grass. Where was the light, where the glory, where the dove?

One of the things Zen masters were acutely aware of was the "stink of Zen." With Yasutani Roshi there was no stink of Zen. However, we must not go to the other extreme and make ordinariness something special or it too will emit the same stink. Some people make a virtue out of being ordinary and then are amazed when someone treats them as just another person.

The koan can be seen as a drama in three acts. The first act: monks on pilgrimage to Gutei, a sacred mountain dedicated to Manjusri, would stop at a tea house for refreshments and then, probably because the road forked, would ask the old woman who served them, "What is the way to Gutei?" She would tell them "Go straight on," and would then add as an aside, "He may be dressed like a monk but he is no different from anyone else." In act two some of the monks who were treated like this tell Joshu, who goes off to investigate the old woman. He arrives, does the same as the monks, asks the same question, receives the same treatment. In act three he goes back to the monks and says, "I've seen into the old woman for you."

The first act has the phrase "Go straight on." How do you go straight on? What does it mean? In English we may speak of a straightforward person, a crooked person, a deviate, an aberrant person. A straightforward person is a clean-cut person, one with no pretenses, who assumes no airs, who is devoid of vanity. It is in this way we must practice, in a straightforward manner, not pretending we are working harder than we are, not pretending we are more advanced than we are, not comparing ourselves with others, not with some ideal image of ourselves or of others as awakened. The implication in the old woman's words is that the monks *do not go straight on*. This is why she says, "He is no better than the rest."

But why does the old woman say the same about Joshu? First let us assume she is also not going straight on, that she too is full of vanity and pretenses, that all she is doing is taking the monks down a peg or two, and that in her eyes Joshu is no different. With this the koan dies. But Mumon likens the old lady and Joshu to two generals: the old lady in her tent planning her strategy, Joshu seeking to infiltrate her defenses. They are evenly matched. We must therefore assume the old lady is deeply awakened. The koan then becomes intriguing. How did Joshu steal into her camp and take the fortress? She saw into Joshu in the same way that Joshu saw into her. But when was this? Come to that, when did Joshu see into the old woman? Mumon gives praise to the woman. She was a general, one who was in charge of the field. But he says she had her faults. Was this because she was taken in? Joshu got right into the enemy's camp, but he too made an error. Was it because he did not take the old woman in? So both had their strengths, both their weaknesses. What were these weaknesses?

Sand in the rice,
Thorns in the mud.

In those times both of these hazards must have been very familiar! One commentary on this koan describes Joshu's question "What is the way to Gutei?" as the sand in the rice, the thorns in the mud. Was it? Or was it Joshu himself?

32 A Non-Buddhist Questions the Buddha

A non-Buddhist once said to the World-Honored One, "Please do not give me words, please do not give me silence." The World-Honored One just sat. The non-Buddhist praised him, "The great compassion of the World-Honored One has opened up the clouds of my ignorance and enabled me to be awakened." Making his bows of gratitude, he departed. Ananda then asked Buddha, "What realization did the non-Buddhist have that made him praise you so much?" The World-Honored One replied, "He is like a high-mettled horse that starts even at the shadow of the whip."

Mumon's Comment

Ananda is Buddha's disciple, yet his realization falls short of the non-Buddhist's. Now tell me, how different are they, the Buddha's disciple and the non-Buddhist?

A Non-Buddhist Questions the Buddha

Mumon's Verse

Walking along the sword's edge,
Running over the ridges of jagged ice,
You need take no step;
Let go your hold on the cliff.

Comment

One of the more noteworthy things about this koan is that a non-Buddhist is the one asking the question and thereby comes to awakening. On the other hand, Ananda, who is one of Buddha's closest disciples, is confused and dismayed by all that happens. The most he could do was ask a perfectly inane question. Awakening is not something confined to Buddhism; it is not even confined to somebody practicing a spiritual way.

If awakening were something confined to people who practice Zen or some other spiritual way, of what use would it be? It would mean that it is bound to some system, not the truth, but a parody of the truth. The rain falls on the just and the unjust alike, and awakening is the birthright of all human beings.

The non-Buddhist had obviously made the rounds of the many teachers available in the time of Buddha, a time of great religious ferment, and he had no doubt heard many conflicting accounts of the spiritual Way. He had probably met with both saints and charlatans, but none had managed to touch his heart. Now he comes to Buddha, probably in desperation. He says, "Please do not give me more words and theories, I've heard and read and discussed too many. But please do not remain silent, silence is of no use." And Buddha just sits there.

Just sitting is *shikantaza* in Japanese, a practice that, in the Yasutani tradition, is not normally allowed until people have passed through the koan practice. As this can take up to fifteen years or more, it means that one would have already been practicing for a long time before starting shikantaza. What is sometimes erroneously taught as shikantaza to beginners is simply looking at the reflection of themselves in the mirror of their minds. Just sitting is possible only when one finally realizes nothing needs to be done, even the least reflection is too much. It normally takes the full fifteen years or more of a great deal of "doing" before the truth of this nothing needs to be done strikes home.

Just sitting does not mean emptying the mind of all thought, or relaxing and letting everything drift; it does not even mean to sit noting, but not being affected by thoughts. All of this entails doing. A short story might help to point up more clearly what just sitting means.

Three men were out for a walk in the country, and up ahead they spied someone sitting on a large rock. To while away a few moments, the three fell to imagining what the stranger was doing. One said he was waiting for a friend, another thought he was resting because he was tired, the third believed he was admiring the view. As they drew close to the stranger one of the three volunteered to approach him and ask what he was doing. He did this, saying, "My friend here says you are waiting for a friend, my other friend says you are resting, and I say you are admiring the view; please, kind sir, tell us what are you doing sitting there?" The stranger said, "I am just sitting."

To most of us this would be tantamount to saying that he is wasting time. People sometimes ask me, "What is the use of zazen?" I always answer, "No use at all!" Everything else may be useful, but not zazen. It is like asking what is the use of the sun shining. Of course many people will say that the sun shining is very useful because without it the plants would not grow and so on. One of my children came home from school with botany notes, one of which stuck firmly in my mind: it said a plant has a stalk to hold the flower up. We must not confuse consequence with use. Many people say that with zazen one gets all kinds of benefits, such as better physical and emotional health, more creativity, and so on. This is the consequence perhaps. But it does not mean that zazen in itself has any use.

> The falling leaves
> Fall and pile up;
> The rain
> Beats on the rain.[8]

What is the use of this piling up, what is the use of rain falling on rain? In his introduction to this koan in the *Hekiganroku*, Engo observes, "It has no form and yet it appears. Filling the ten directions; it is boundless. It responds spontaneously, arises in emptiness." This reminds one of the saying of Buddha, "There is that sphere wherein is neither earth nor water, fire nor air: it is not the infinity of space, nor the infinity of perception; it is not nothingness, nor is it neither idea nor non-idea; it is neither this world nor the next, nor is it both; it is neither the sun nor the moon. It neither comes nor goes, it neither abides nor passes away; it is not caused, established, begun, supported; it is the end of suffering." Both Buddha and Engo could have added, "yet it is entirely useless." It is the end of suffering because it is the end of the eternal search for the useful, in which everything becomes an instrument.

Suffering is the cause of practice, but we should not turn practice into a technique for ending suffering.

[8] From *Zen Forest*, trans. by Sōiku Shigematsu.

Suffering, as Buddha said, is the basis of life; we suffer because we wish to exist, to be something in the world, and in seeking to be something we use everything in support of this search, and we use everything to overcome the suffering that is entailed in this search. Fear of death is the realization that ultimately no security is possible, that all our some-things must come to an end. With this a new kind of suffering can come into being that originates in a yearning to find our way back home. If we practice to bring an end to our suffering we may well bring an end to the practice itself. It is suffering coming from yearning to return home that Buddha refers to when he says in reply to Ananda's question, "He is like a high-mettled horse that starts at even the shadow of the whip."

In the Buddhist scriptures it says, "The one who reflects upon the transience of life when he learns someone in another village is about to die is like a high-mettled horse that starts even at the shadow of the whip. The one who reflects upon the transience of life only when he learns that someone in his own village is about to die is like a horse who runs when it is whipped. The one who reflects upon the transience of life only when he learns that someone in his own family is about to die is like a horse who runs when it is flogged. And finally, the one who reflects upon the transience of life only when he learns that he himself is about to die is like a horse who runs when it is flogged to the bone."

Ananda took many years to come to awakening, the non-Buddhist came to awakening in a moment. Mumon asks, "Ananda is Buddha's disciple, yet his understanding falls short of the non-Buddhist's. Now tell me, how different are they, the Buddha's disciple and the non-Buddhist?" One has it, the other doesn't; both are unique, no difference can be found.

33 Baso's "No Mind, No Buddha"

A monk asked Baso, "What is Buddha?" Baso answered, "No mind, no Buddha."

Mumon's Comment

See into this and you have finished your practice of Zen.

Mumon's Verse

If you meet a swordsman, give him a sword;
Only give a poem to a poet.
When talking, tell one third of it;
Don't divulge the whole at once.

34 Nansen's "Reason Is Not the Way"

Nansen said, "Mind is not the Buddha; knowing is not the Way."

Mumon's Comment

Nansen, growing old, lost his shame. Just opening his stinking mouth he revealed all the family secrets. Yet there are few who are grateful for his kindness.

Mumon's Verse

The sky clears, the sun shines bright;
The rain falls, the earth gets wet.
He opens his heart and expounds the whole secret.
But I fear he is little appreciated.

Comment

Huang Po once said to his monks, "There is only one mind and not an iota of anything else that one can grasp, for *this mind is Buddha*. If you who are practicing the Way do not awaken to the reality of mind, you will cover mind with conceptual thought, you will seek Buddha outside yourselves." In koan 30 Baso states categorically, "This very mind is Buddha." In the previous koan he says, "No mind, no Buddha." Buddha is mind, Buddha is not mind, mind is not mind, Buddha is not Buddha. What is going on here?

Arthur Koestler asked the same question when, after quoting D.T. Suzuki as saying "ugly is beautiful, false is true, and also conversely," he went into the attack saying, "the perversions of Pop-Zen are based on juggling with the identity of opposites, the Communists juggling with the dialectics of history, the Schoolmen on a combination of Holy Scripture with Aristotelian logic. The axioms differ, but the delusional process follows much the same pattern. Facts and arguments which succeed in penetrating the outer defenses are processed by the dialectical method until 'false' becomes 'true,' tyranny becomes true democracy, and a herring a racehorse."[9]

If Koestler had been a little more careful, and perhaps a little more charitable, he would have seen that his accusations, at least as far as Suzuki was concerned, were not just. On the other hand, it must be said the kind of rhetoric he is attacking is not uncommon in Zen literature, and Koestler is right when he says it can be dangerous. Just as we are not to destroy moral conduct based on rules, but go beyond it in an ever sensitive response to situations, so we are not to destroy logic but to live in a wider reason that contains but is not limited by it.

[9.] *The Ghost in the Machine* by Arthur Koestler (New York: Viking Penguin, 1990).

A monk asked Baso why he said mind is Buddha. Baso answered, "Because I want to stop the crying of babes." The monk persisted, "When the crying has stopped, what then?" Baso said, "Not mind, not Buddha." The monk asked, "How would you deal with the man that does not uphold either of these two view points?" Baso said, "I would tell him, not things." The monk went on, "If you met a man free from all attachments, what would you tell him?" The master replied, "I would let him enjoy the great Way." Each of these answers is appropriate to the moment, but they do not differ basically from one another. Buddha did not teach the truth, but *the way to the truth.* He said when one has reached the other shore then this teaching should be abandoned.

Nansen's "Mind is not Buddha; knowing is not the Way" is Joshu's "Mu!" When the old man in Hyakujo's Fox declares, "I am not a human being," one must resist the temptation to ask, "Well, what are you?" So in a similar way, one must not turn around to Nansen and say, "If it is not mind or knowing, what is it?" The *Prajnaparamita* speaks of the Bodhisattva "holding to nothing whatever," but we must not conceive of this nothing being the opposite of something. This nothing has no ontological status. According to Mumon's verse,

> *The sky clears, the sun shines bright;*
> *The rain comes, the earth gets wet.*

"Nothing whatever" is clarity with not a speck of dust anywhere. It is completely transparent. In the same way everything is revealed in Nansen's, "Mind is not the Buddha; knowing is not the Way." This koan is elaborated on in the following story.

Nansen's "Reason is Not the Way"

On one occasion Nansen said, "Ma-tsu of Kiangsi maintained mind is Buddha. However, I would not say it this way. I would advocate not mind, not Buddha, not things. Is there any mistake when I say it in this way?" After listening to this Joshu made a bow and went away. Thereupon a monk followed him, calling, "What did you mean just now when you bowed and left the master?" Joshu replied, "Sir, you will have to ask the master." The monk went to the master and inquired, "Why did Joshu behave that way a moment ago?" "He understood my meaning!" Nansen exclaimed.

Mumon says further,

He opens his heart and expounds the whole secret.
But I fear he is little appreciated.

If it took Mumon six hard years to appreciate it, we should not wonder that Nansen is not well appreciated. But on second thought, who is Nansen, and where was Joshu when he bowed?

35 Sei and Her Soul

*G*oso said to his monks, "Sei and her soul are separated. Who is the true Sei?"

Mumon's Comment

When you realize who the real one is, then you will see that coming out of one husk and going into another is like a traveler putting up at hotels. If you have not yet realized it, do not rush about blindly. When suddenly earth, water, fire, and air disintegrate, you will be like a crab that has fallen into boiling water, struggling with its seven arms and eight legs. Do not say that I have not warned you.

Mumon's Verse

Ever the same the moon among the clouds;
Different from each other, the mountain and the valley.

Sei and Her Soul

Wonderful, wonderful, wonderful.
Is this one, or two?

The Story

This koan is based on a popular love story of the time, a sort of Chinese Romeo and Juliet. Once upon a time in a place called Koyo, a man whose name was Chokan lived with his daughter Sei. She was very beautiful, and her father loved her very much. She had a handsome cousin named Ochu, and Chokan used to joke that they would make a fine pair. The two young people took his joking seriously, and, being in love with each other, considered themselves engaged. However, the father wanted to give Sei in marriage to another young man, Hinryo, and tragedy seemed inevitable.

Ochu was indignant when he heard about Chokan's decision, and left the place by boat. After several days at sea he found to his astonishment that Sei was with him on the boat. Overjoyed, he took her to the country of Shoku where they lived for several years and had two children.

Sei, however, could not forget her native land. She regretted having deserted her father and wondered what he was thinking of her. So her husband encouraged her to return home and decided to go back with her. When they arrived at the father's house, Ochu asked Sei to remain at the boat while he went to her father to apologize for what had happened. "What are you talking about?" exclaimed the father. "Who is this woman you are talking about?" "It is Sei," replied Ochu. "Nonsense!" said Chokan. "Sei became ill and has been in bed for several years. That is not Sei at all!" Ochu went back to the boat and brought Sei to the father's house. Then the Sei who was lying in bed, being told of this, when Sei came from the boat, arose from her bed and went to her and the two became one.

Comment

A koan not found in the *Mumonkan* might help in arousing the mind on the Sei koan. Two sisters were out in the rain; which is the one who did not get wet?

Plato tells of a myth in which at one time the earth was populated by beings with four legs, four arms and hands, and two heads. They were so strong and self-assured that the gods became afraid that they would take over heaven. So they sliced these beings in half, "like a flat fish," Plato said. Ever since then each half has sought its other half. This is the myth of romantic love, but it is also a myth of all love. Originally we are one and whole. But we become divided within ourselves in such a way that only half is ever able to find satisfaction, one half searches forever to find its soul mate to become whole again.

On the one hand, we want to go out and conquer the world, do things, travel, meet new and interesting people. On the other hand we long for a quiet life, walks in the country, meditation, peace. If we break away from it all and find a place in the country, primitive but peaceful, within a short while we long to be back in the hustle and bustle of things. And when we are back we think with nostalgia of the peace we once knew. Life seems to oscillate between boredom, after we have shucked off as many responsibilities as we can, and tension, when we have involved ourselves over our heads once more.

But have you experienced that magical moment when you feel totally at one with another person? There seems to be more space, more light in his or her presence. For a while the tension of being just oozes out, and one is left in life and light.

Love is not homogenous. Many different kinds of love are to be found, human love and love of the divine. There is possessive love, love that wants to absorb, smother, control; and submissive, dependent love that wants to surrender to be cared for, comforted, and given security. There is also a love where the welfare of the other is all that matters; it is not altruistic, it has no great ideal to support it; it is pure generosity; sometimes it borders on the possessive. Finally, there is adoration, seeing in the other the whole, the all; this is not idolatry but rather an absence of self in the presence of another.

Rarely is just one kind of love present, rarely are we sufficiently pure in heart that we can, in Kierkegaard's words, "will one thing." As humans we are complex, and this complexity colors all that we do. But even so, beyond the complexity and the confusion, the muddled fog of existence is *that* which is common to all kinds of love. It is said "God is love," and if it were not such a cliché that would say it all. Common to all love, including sexual and divine love, is original unity, the unity alluded to in Plato's myth. Originally we are one, but subsequently we are divided in two and from this two comes multiplicity. The different forms of love are like the spectrum that pure light breaks into when it passes thorough a prism of glass. When the light of unity passes through the prism of the human heart it too breaks down into a spectrum, and human life is colored by it.

Mumon expresses the spirit of this koan in his verse.

Ever the same the moon among the clouds;
Different from each other, the mountain and the valley.
Wonderful, wonderful, wonderful.
Is this one, or two?

Duality in unity, *unus-ambo* as it is called in the Sufi tradition, is at the basis of all religion. In the Gnostic religion, the religion of knowing, it appears frequently. For example, a Christian Gnostic poem reads:

I am the first and the last.
I am the honored one and the scorned one.
I am the whore and the holy one.
I am the wife and the virgin.
I am (the mother) and the daughter.
I am she whose wedding is great and
I have not taken a husband. [10]

The Gospel of St. Thomas reads:

When you make the two one
and make the inside like the outside
and the outside like the inside
and the upper side like the underside
and in such a way that you make the man with the
*   woman a single one in such a way that the man is*
*   not man and the woman is not woman;*
then you will go into the kingdom.[11]

The moon is one, the mountains and the valley are different from each other and are two. The moon is one, the mountains and valleys are one. Mumon asks is this one, is this two? Ambiguity is what the koan is about: oneness and twoness, oneness that is twoness, oneness that is not even oneness.

Sei and her soul are separated; which is the true Sei? On the one hand is Sei the recluse, at home, turned in on herself. On the other is Sei the mother and wife, the extrovert joining in life, and at home in the world. Which is the

[10] *The Gnostic Gospels* by Elaine Papels.
[11] *The Secret Sayings of Jesus* by Robert M. Grant.

true Sei? The Gnostic text simply stated the problem with no thought of its resolution. The text of St. Thomas suggests a merging, making two into one, a mystical marriage. But neither one is the Way of Zen. A Sufi poem written by Ib'n Arabi comes close to the spirit of Zen:

If then you perceive me, you perceive yourself.
But you cannot perceive me through yourself.
It is through my eyes that you see me and see your self,
Through your eyes you cannot see me.

Zen Master Yoka said:

Delusions need not be removed;
Truth need not be sought after.
The reality of ignorance is one with Buddha nature;
The illusory form is one with the dharma body.

36 When You Meet a Man of the Way

G oso said, "When you meet a man of the Way on the way, do not greet him with words do not greet him with silence. Tell me how will you greet him?"

Mumon's Comment
If you can have an intimate meeting with him you are to be congratulated. But if you cannot, you must be present at every step.

Mumon's Verse
> Meeting a man of the Way on the road,
> Meet him with neither words nor silence.
> A punch on the jaw:
> Understand if you can directly.

Comment

Who is the man or woman of the Way? Given Mumon's verse, it seems that you are walking along and you meet someone, and you give him or her a punch on the jaw and continue on. It all seems terribly violent. However, we must remember Mumon's earlier comment, "If you meet the Buddha, kill the Buddha; if you met the patriarchs, kill the patriarchs." Obviously none of this can be taken literally, but even so, why is the language so violent?

A story is told of one of the desert fathers who was meditating for a long time alone. One day the Archangel Gabriel came in a blaze of light to see him. The angel said, "I have come to reward you for the devotion that you have shown." The anchorite replied, "I'm afraid you have made a big mistake. Will you please go away."

In many traditions to meet Buddha, or to meet an angel, to meet one on the Way is a great achievement. So-called channeling is a method by which some people deliberately stimulate their minds to produce visions of higher beings and so claim contact with them. Sometimes the "higher being" is a vision of a being of light, a vision sometimes encountered by people who have come near to death. A society has been formed to enable these people to meet and communicate with others who are interested in the phenomena produced. Some of these people have even taken on the role of prophet or seer. However, as Mumon affirms, in Zen practice if one meets one on the Way, cut that one down.

One of the dangers that comes with these visions is that of becoming attached to them. The practice of having "experiencers" as they are called, that is people who have had a near-death experience, parade themselves and this experience before hundreds of others at conferences and conventions is dangerous, at least as far as the spiritual life of the experiencer is concerned. Any such experience, however exalted, is only an experience and, as with all such experiences, it drifts away into the twilight of the past. Whatever insight comes from it becomes conceptualized and frozen along with all the other concepts and ideas that litter the mind. Exalting the experience encourages its own form of egoism. This is why Mumon recommends the punch on the jaw, and if someone meets the Buddha, kill the Buddha. The attraction is so powerful it requires an equally powerful antidote.

When we practice Zen we meet the one on the Way, sometimes in a beatific form but sometimes in a horrific form. This horrific form emerges because we see into true nature, but, as it were, through a glass darkly, through concepts, prejudices, and theories. Then the serenity of emptiness can become the lonely hell of nothingness; we are swallowed in the maw of our own swallowing like a snake that swallows its own tail. In Zen this is called *makyo,* and to practice one must neither flee from the fearful nor cling to the exalted. If you meet one on the way, do not greet him with words, do not greet him with silence. How would you greet him?

37 Joshu's Oak Tree

"*W*hat is the meaning of Bodhidharma's coming from the West?*"*

"*The oak tree in the garden.*"

Mumon's Comment

If you can see into Joshu's answer immediately, there is no Shakya before you, no Maitreya to come.

Mumon's Verse

Words cannot express things,
Speech does not convey the spirit.
Swayed by words, one is lost;
Blocked by phrases, one is bewildered.

Comment

This koan is probably taken from the time when Joshu had

completed his pilgrimage. After his first awakening he stayed with Nansen for about forty years until Nansen's death. He then went on a pilgrimage for twenty years, and only then, at the age of eighty, did he settle down in one place to teach; he died at the age of one hundred and twenty.

Joshu was not a fire eater like Ummon, Rinzai, and Tokusan. One has the impression of a gentle, highly intelligent man with a wry sense of irony. A number of mondo have been collected involving him.

Someone asked him, "What is my essence?" He said, "The tree sways, the bird flies about, the fish leaps, the water is muddy."

On another occasion he was asked, "When Buddha was alive the people found deliverance in him. Now Buddha is no more, where should the people turn to?" "There is no such thing as the people," Joshu said. "But," protested the monk, "Am I not here asking?" "If so, what Buddha are you looking for?" retorted Joshu.

Someone sprang the question on him, "The right in front of the eyes Buddha—what is it?"

"The Buddha in the main hall."

"That is a physical Buddha. What is Buddha?"

"It is mind."

"If you define it as mind you limit it. What is Buddha?"

"It is no-mind."

"You say mind you say no-mind, am I allowed to choose?"

"Mind and no-mind, it was all your choice. Is there anything you want me to say that will satisfy you?"

Someone asked a master, "What is the most important

question?" The master replied, "It is the one you ask with the mouth closed." The real question, what T.S. Eliot called the overwhelming question, cannot be asked with words. That is why very often the ritual question is asked in Zen mondo: what is Buddha? What is the meaning of Bodhidharma's coming from the West? Often in life we are completely nonplussed. Someone dies or leaves us, we fall seriously ill, or we lose our jobs and we are stunned. Buried deep in this stunning is a question, but how can we ask it? We stammer, "What is the meaning of life? Why was I born? Who am I? What is death?" But these are far from what the real issue is about.

The great pilgrimage to awakening undertaken by Buddha had its start in the shock he received after several encounters: first with a sick man, then with an old man, and finally with a dead man. Buddha's response to this shock was to undertake six long and arduous years of austerity and spiritual search. Talking about spiritual search often brings up another question, that, although it is based on the first unaskable question and so in its turn is unaskable, goes far beyond it: What does spiritual work mean? This question is couched in the monk's ritual question, "What is the meaning of Bodhidharma's coming from the West?"

Let us nevertheless try to ask, what is spiritual work, what is a spiritual person, and what is spirituality? Many people think in terms of goodness, and in their endeavor to be known as a spiritual person become a "good" person. The typical picture of Jesus is of a handsome, blondish young man looking up to heaven out of gentle eyes; the whip-cracking, enraged consort of prostitutes and the world's downtrodden can hardly be recognized in this ethereal gaze. If it is not goodness that is brought to mind by the question about spirituality, it is charisma. So often people confuse charisma with wisdom, but how often do we hear that the highly charismatic person turns out after all to be a rogue. In truth, no spiritual person has ever existed. This among other things is inherent in Joshu's response.

What was the meaning of Bodhidharma's coming to the West? Yasutani used to say if Bodhidharma's coming had some meaning, in fact, if he had brought anything with him, he would not have been worth a cent. When someone asked Dogen what he had found during his stay in China he replied: "My eyes are horizontal and my nose is vertical."

In koan 20 in the *Hekiganroku* a monk, Ryuge, asked another monk, Suibi, "What is the meaning of Bodhidharma's coming from the West?" Suibi requested that Ryuge pass a sitting cushion to him. When Ryuge did so, Suibi hit him with it. Ryuge said, "You can hit me if you like, but after all, Bodhidharma's coming from the West has no meaning." This performance was repeated when Ryuge asked Rinzai the same question. Again Ryuge was struck with the cushion and again, using identical words, Ryuge said, "You can hit me if you like but, after all, Bodhidharma's coming from the West has no meaning." To say "no meaning" is one thing, to say this no meaning has no meaning is something else.

At first glance Joshu's reply here seems to be the same as Tosan's "three pounds of flax." However, the two responses have a great deal that is different. It is the very thereness of the tree that is at issue for Joshu. His response is not unlike Van Gogh's irises or Cezanne's apples. To know the irises as Van Gogh knew them, or the apples as Cezanne knew them, one must be the irises, be the apples. In Zen it is said one should sit like an oak tree with its roots deep into the ground, its branches lost in the sky, immutable, whole. If one has done this one will have no difficulty with Joshu's oak tree in the garden, and one will know the radical difference between thereness and over-thereness.

Mumon says, "If you can see into Joshu's answer immediately, there is no Shakya before you, no Maitreya to come." There is not even an oak tree!

I am told that at the entrance to many Rinzai monasteries one encounters the admonition, "Look under your feet!" Joshu's oak tree is everywhere.

38 A Buffalo Passes Through a Window

*G*oso said, *"A buffalo passes through the window. His head, horns, four legs all go through. But why can't the tail go through also?"*

Mumon's Comment

If you can make a complete turnabout, open your Zen eye, and utter a turning word on this, you will be able to repay the four obligations and help the sentient beings in the three realms who follow you. If you are still unable to do this, return to this tail and reflect upon it, and then for the first time you will grasp it.

Mumon's Verse

Passing through, it falls into a ditch;
Going back, it is lost.
This tiny tail,
What a strange thing it is!

Comment

It is easy to demonstrate this koan, but difficult to plumb to its depths. It can be looked at from a purely exoteric point of view or from a deeper, more hidden point of view.

Have you ever noticed how the apple always seems to have a worm in it? It is like being in a comfortable bed, warm and snug except for a crease in the pillow, a bump in the mattress, or an itch in the leg. Each time one thing is settled another comes up.

"How's your new job?" "It's great, really, I like it. The only thing is there is this fellow who never stops talking. . . ."

"How was your holiday?" "We've never had a better one, but the people next door were so noisy. . . ."

"How was the party?" "It was wonderful, but guess who was there!"

No doubt one day it will be, "How do you like paradise?" "It's heavenly but these halos are so tight."

Many people have this "if only" feeling about themselves, about their bodies, about their personalities: if only I were taller, shorter, thinner, fatter, had a bigger nose, a smaller nose. If only I were more outgoing, less noisy, more loving, more independent. Everything is fine, the head, horns, four legs, and body all have got through. But that tail. If only. . . !

Deeper yet is another view of the tail; or rather it is the same view seen from within rather than from without. This view will be familiar to those who have sat for a long time in meditation. After years of struggle the thoughts are no longer important, the feelings are at peace, the posture no longer obtrudes; clarity and vastness are present, but so is the observer, so am "I." It seems if I go forward I will fall into an abyss of oblivion; if I go back I find myself lost once more in a shower of thoughts and dreams. But I cannot stay where I am. Again it is Hakuin's rat in a bamboo tube. This tiny tail, what a strange thing it is!

Mumon tells us we must make a complete about-face and open the wisdom eye. This turnabout must be made within the I itself. In Zen it is said, "The thief my child." In a similar vein a nun complained that she could not pull up the weed because if she did she would pull up the flower with it. The problem is not how to get rid of I, but how to throw the bath water away without losing the baby.

What is this I? As one works on this question it ultimately seems nothing more than a viewpoint. Nisargadatta likened it to a pinpoint hole in a sheet of paper. It is *in* the paper but not *of* the paper. Furthermore, its presence is its absence. The more one denies it, the more one affirms it, because denial requires a viewpoint no less than affirmation. This viewpoint is often taken to be the real self, although this cannot be because in sleep we put it aside. However, this viewpoint is the tiny tail, and within it we must make the turnabout that Mumon speaks of.

In Sanskrit the viewpoint is called the *manas*. It is from this word that words such as man and mind have been derived. So it is in the manas that the turnabout, or, again using the Sanskrit word, *paravritti*, must be made. It is a turnabout from seeing the world to being the world, from knowing *something* to knowing.

Our difficulty is that to see we must separate, that is unless we can see without eyes, and yet, as the Jesuit Teillard de Chardin, observed, "To be is to see." Everything that lives and moves is a viewpoint. The ant, the bee, the flea, the horse, the elephant, and the giraffe. To be is to see, and to see is to be separate, and to be separate is to fear the whole, because the whole is seen as death and annihilation. Sometimes it is said that "coming home" is for the drop to be merged with the whole; at other times it is said that the whole must be merged into the drop. But Goso wants to push us further still.

In Goso's statement, on the one hand is the buffalo, on the other the tail, two parts. But the whole is not the buffalo on which a tail has been added, although we seem to see it like that when we fear the whole. The whole is not even a whole buffalo. Some blind men were studying a buffalo. One said it was like a thin trunk of a tree, he was holding its leg; another said it was like a big barrel, he was feeling its body; another said it was cold like stone, he was feeling its horn; another said it was like a rope, he was holding it tail. One who had eyes came along and laughed because he saw the whole buffalo. But even he did not have the last laugh. This last laugh is reserved for the tenth person, the one who has an open eye and is blind.

39 Ummon Said, "You Missed!"

A monk said to Ummon, "The radiance serenely illumines the whole universe. . . ." Before he could finish the line, Ummon interrupted him and asked, "Aren't those the words of Chosetsu?" The monk said, "Yes, they are." Ummon said, "You missed." Later the master Shishin took up this matter and asked, "Tell me, how did the monk miss?"

Mumon's Comment

If you can see how uncompromising and rigorous is Ummon's method and how the monk missed, then you qualify as teacher of people and gods. If it is not yet clear then you cannot save even yourself.

Mumon's Verse

A line is cast in the swift stream;
The greedy will be caught;

If your mouth opens just a bit,
You will lose your life completely.

Comment

The monk was quoting the awakening verse of Chosetsu.
The whole verse reads as follows:

Serenely radiance illumines the whole universe;
The ignorant, the wise, all dwell in one abode.
When no thought arises, One is revealed;
If the six sense organs move just a little, it is covered
  by clouds.
Cutting off ignorance causes it to grow;
Looking for truth is of no avail.
Living at one with things of the world creates no
  problem;
Nirvana and life-and-death are like flowers of air.

What is this radiance that serenely illumines the whole
universe? Jesus said we are the light of the world. That
seems to be what Chosetsu said. But even so, what is this
light of the world? It is not one that we can see but rather
one *by which* we see. Everything comes into its own within
this light. But the moment we try to find the light through
seeing or hearing, it is covered up in its own reflection.
Trying to correct this by study and thought, or trying to
overcome ignorance by seeking to know this radiance in
experience, even in spiritual experience, simply makes matters worse. Living according to things, being one with all
that happens, making no separation of this and that, mine
and yours, mine and his, everything become a dharma gate.
We then realize awakening is to see no awakening is neces-

sary and that life and death are the very forms of the radiance itself.

The monk was lost in a welter of words. He wanted to find the whole by asking a question about it, using another's words. But whose words were they really? Were they Chosetsu's? After the fall of France during World War II, Churchill gave a speech to his countrymen in which he said, "All I can offer you is blood, tears, toil, and sweat." I was twelve years old when I heard those words, but they have never left me. And they galvanized the British public. What had been a demoralized, fragmented nation became a whole. Whose words were they? Churchill of course chose them, but once he delivered them they belonged to all who heard them in Britain at the time.

A master said when you have the meaning you can throw away the words. The monk did not have the meaning and so was clinging to the words. He understood undoubtedly the meaning of the *words*. But the meaning of what Chosetsu said was not in the words, it was in the radiance that serenely illumines the whole universe; when you have that, or when you are that, what do you want with words?

40 Isan Kicks Over the Jug

When Isan was practicing with Hyakujo, he was appointed as head cook at the monastery. Hyakujo wanted to choose an abbot for a monastery at Daii. He called together the head monk and the rest of his disciples to have them demonstrate their insight; the most adept would be sent to found the monastery. He took a jug, put it on the floor, and asked: "Don't call this a jug, what is it?" The head monk objected," You can't call it a clog." Hyakujo then asked Isan. Isan walked over, kicked over the jug and left. Hyakujo said to the head monk, "You have been defeated by Isan." Isan was ordered to start the monastery.

Mumon's Comment

Extremely valiant though he is, Isan could not after all get out of Hyakujo's trap. If one considers it carefully, he chose

what is heavy, refused what is light. Why? Taking the towel
from his head, he put on an iron yoke.

Mumon's Verse

> *Throwing away bamboo baskets and wooden ladles,*
> *With one direct blow he cuts off complications.*
> *Hyakujo tries to stop him with his strict barrier, but in*
> *vain.*
> *The tip of his foot creates innumerable Buddhas.*

Comment

Don't call this a jug, what is it? It seems a strange question
when we first hear it. We are so used to associating words
and things that when we take away the word we are confused. What remains when the word has been taken away?
The head monk evidently thought that something remained,
something with all the characteristics of a jug but lacking
just the name. "You can't call it a clog," he says. Evidently
not, because a clog does not have that shape, that size, those
characteristics. But Isan kicked over the jug. The whole
question of course is why? Why does doing that enable Isan
to walk right through the trap that Hyakujo had set up?

The monk evidently saw words as labels, as things one
sticks on other things. This is a common view. However,
words are only labels after they have lost their generative
power. Before this they bring things into being. The generative power is illustrated in Genesis: "God said, 'Let there be
light,'" as well as in the ending of Christian prayers: "in the
name of the Father and of the Son and of the Holy Ghost."

The abracadabra of the stage magician is a vague
reminder of the close connection between magic and words.
It is said that to control the devil, one must name the devil.

Because of their power, names have always had a certain amount of taboo around them. This is why one must not take the Lord's name in vain. A psychologist who had twin daughters wrote of how one day he mistakenly called each by the other's name. At first the twins thought this a great joke, but as he persisted, they became worried, then anxious, and eventually panicky. There is also the story of a woman with schizophrenia: she would have bouts of panic and fear when objects seemed to look at her with malevolence, and the only way she could control her fear was to call out the names of the objects.

We have the impression that the world is made up of things, but this world of things is derived from a deeper, unified world, a world of *immediate experience*. Fundamental to the Buddha's teaching is the doctrine of *anicca*, which is summed up in the words of a Zen master, "From the beginning not a thing is." Put differently, our psychic life does not begin with things but with immediate experience. The nineteenth-century British philosopher F.H. Bradley observed that "in the beginning there are no relations and no feelings, but only differences that work and are felt but not discriminated. . . . The total state is an immediate feeling, a knowing and being in one." He pointed out also that feeling does not mean mere sensation or feelings such as pleasure and pain; rather, it is immediate experience without any distinction or relation in itself. "It is unity complex but without relations. Feeling is not one differentiated aspect but holds all aspects in one."[12]

Some similarity exists between Bradley's comment and what Hyakujo once said: "By the ineffable subtlety of thinking without thinking, turn your attention inward to reflect upon the infinite power of the divine spark. When your

[12] *Studies in the Metaphysics of Bradley* by Sushil Kumar Saxena.

thinking can go no further it returns to the source, the eternal home of nature and form, where phenomena and noumenon are not dual but one, there abides the Suchness of the true Buddha." On hearing these words, Isan came to awakening. Hyakujo was prompting Isan to go beyond immediate experience referred to by Bradley, beyond what is better known in Buddhism as samadhi. The ineffable subtlety of thinking without thinking is another way of saying *arouse the mind without resting it upon anything,* on any kind of experience immediate or mediated by words, thoughts, ideas, or feelings. Even so, Bradley gives us a direction in which to look, and the direction is given moreover by a modern Westerner who probably had no knowledge of or interest in Buddhism.

We can see more clearly now the quandary into which Hyakujo plunged Isan, "Don't call this a jug, what is it?" or we could say, "Don't use words, what is left?" And Isan kicks over the jug. The real question now is how does he do this? Does he give it kick like a soccer player belting a ball? Does he trip over it? Does he kick with disgust? Mumon's verse goes, "With a one direct blow he cuts off complications."

41 Bodhidharma Sets the Mind at Rest

*B*odhidharma sat facing the wall. The second patriarch, having cut off his arm, stood there in the snow. He said, "Your disciple's mind is not yet at peace. I beg the master to give it rest." Bodhidharma replied, "Bring your mind and I will give it rest." The patriarch said, "I have searched for that mind, and can find it nowhere." Bodhidharma said, "Then I have given it rest."

Mumon's Comment

The broken-toothed old foreigner crossed thousands of miles of sea, raising waves where no wind blew. He had but one disciple, and even that disciple had only one arm. Well! Well!

Mumon's Verse

> *Coming from the West and directly pointing:*
> *All our troubles come from that!*

Bodhidharma Sets the Mind at Rest

All the monks being at sixes and sevens
Comes from these two chaps.

Comment

Bodhidharma is the first Chinese patriarch of Zen. He is also incidentally the first patriarch of the martial arts, and his temple at Shao-ling is a pilgrimage center not for Zen Buddhists but for those practicing the martial arts. He is celebrated for his insistence on direct pointing to the human heart, nonreliance on words and letters.

Among the few pieces of writing attributed to him is one called, "The Rule of the Requital of Hatred." It reads as follows:

If a follower of the Way should fall into times of trial or suffering, that one should think and say this:

During countless past ages I have abandoned the root and gone after the branches, carried along on the restless, bitter waves of the sea of existence and thereby creating endless occasions for hate, ill will and wrong doing. The harm done has been limitless. Although my present suffering is not caused by any wrong doing committed in this life, yet it is the fruit of my sins in my past existence which happens to ripen at this moment. It is not something which men or gods have given to me. Let me therefore take patiently and sweetly this bitter fruit of my own making without resentment or complaint against anyone. When the mind is awakened it responds spontaneously to the dictates of reason so that it can make use of other people's hatred and turn it into an occasion for an advance toward the Tao.

This koan tells of his encounter with Hui K'o who became the second patriarch. Hui K'o had come to Bodhidharma for his teaching, but Bodhidharma had rejected him, saying, "The subtle and supreme teachings of the Buddhas can only be pursued by endless travail, doing what is hard to do and bearing what is hard to bear, continuing the practice for kalpas; how can a man of little virtue and much self-conceit dream of achieving it? It will end only in fruitless labor." However, Hui K'o persisted and eventually cut off his arm to show his sincerity. Because of this, Bodhidharma relented.

One must not take the statement about the second patriarch having cut off his arm too literally. To cut off one's arm would be a most amazing feat unless one had an extremely sharp sword, and then one would have to worry about all the blood. It is an interesting fact that in English we have the expression "I would give my right arm for. . . ." and the blank is filled by the particular good for which we would relinquish the limb. To give up one's right arm is to give up one's power to act.

What we must see in Hui K'o is a man at the end of his tether, who even before cutting it off had already given his right arm. He has tried everything to reach some understanding, to get some idea of what it is all about. Finally, he hears about this remarkable old man, over one hundred years old, who has left the security of his native home and traveled across the ocean to bring some light to China; who, on arriving, has an interview with the emperor and, instead of playing the sycophant, virtually snubs the ruler and walks off to sit alone in a cave. Here at last Hui K'o has the opportunity he has prayed for: here is a man who is authentic and knowledgeable, and who must want to share his understanding with others in that he was willing to face considerable danger crossing the sea to reach China.

He goes to Bodhidharma, who simply rejects him out of hand, laughing at him, saying his half-hearted efforts are no use whatsoever. But Hui K'o does not budge. He knows that if he leaves, the one opportunity that life has offered will never be repeated. He simply has to see and talk to this man. So he stands outside the cave waiting for Bodhidharma to accept him. As he stands outside it starts to snow. It goes on snowing, but still he stands there. Still Bodhidharma sits resolutely facing the wall, not moving. The snow comes down and Hui K'o stands there.

Eventually Hui K'o cuts off his arm and Bodhidharma relents. It is impossible for a teacher to resist someone who is genuine. Such a person, one who will indeed give his right arm, is above all what the teacher is looking for. Then Hui K'o begs, "My mind is not at peace, please give it peace."

How can Bodhidharma respond to this poor man, shivering, hungry, in physical and mental pain? In the *Dharmapadda*, a basic Buddhist text, it says,

> By oneself evil is done,
> By oneself one suffers.
> By oneself evil is undone,
> No one can purify another.

No one can purify another, and yet the heart-wrenching call for peace to his mind must have struck Bodhidharma to his very marrow. He simply tells Hui K'o to give him his mind and he would set it at rest. Was this but a way of avoiding the issue? Was Bodhidharma giving Hui K'o an impossible task so he would go away knowing he could not be helped, that he had to find the way himself?

On the contrary, it was an act of supreme courage and compassion. Would not most of us have wanted to give consoling words, sympathy, or encouragement?

One thing the koan does is underline the kind of commitment required for the practice of Zen, and the selflessness required to teach Zen. But let us put the commitment into perspective. Many people, when they hear of the dedication necessary to come to awakening, become discouraged, complaining, "I could never do that!" Yet Shibayama says, "I shall never forget the spiritual struggle I had in sheer darkness for nearly three years. I would declare that what is most important and invaluable in Zen training is this experience of dark nights that one goes through with one's whole being." My own experience confirms this. For about four years I was in a no-man's-land of pure pain and anguish without any sense of direction or any idea if the journey would ever end. My only faith was in zazen. The Way is not the way of a hero; this dark night of the soul is not something that one enters into intentionally, but rather, as one lets go of the various illusory values that one has, so one lets go of all the artificial light that has lit up one's way. But even in the darkness is a feeling of the rightness of the way; even in the pain is a peace coming from knowing one is on the Way.

If you ask someone who is on the Way, "Why are you practicing?" the answer you may well hear is, "I don't know, I simply have to go on," or some variation of this. Indeed, one could say if a person does know, he or she is not very far on the Way. In the early days of my training, going to sesshin was sheer hell. Several days beforehand I would be tense, anxious, and distracted. I would dread the journey to the center, but even so I had to go. The practice has nothing for the personality, which often is threatened and disturbed by it. Something much more profound is at work. If one persists despite the travail, at a certain stage in the practice the frustrations, conflicts, and defects suffered by the personality become the fuel driving the practice forward. It is during this time that, in spite of oneself, one can make immense efforts that in sober moments seem impossible. Thus we must never put ourselves down, to do so is to put down Buddha nature, which is the source and power of practice.

Hui K'o, when he in turn became a teacher, quoted the Hwa Yen: "It is as vast as the universe, as ultimate as the void. But it is also like a light in a jar that cannot illuminate the outside." He went on, "When learners rely on written and spoken words on the path, these are like a lamp in the wind: they cannot dispel darkness, and their flame dies away. But if learners sit in purity without concerns, it is like a lamp in a closed room: it can dispel the darkness, and it illuminates things with clarity."

But to sit in purity: what a struggle it takes. As Rinzai described it, "Years ago when I was not enlightened I was in sheer darkness altogether." Hakuin observed, "I felt as though I was sitting in an ice cave ten thousand miles thick." Shibayama chastised, "You who have not spent sleepless nights in suffering and tears, who do not know the experience of being unable to swallow even a piece of bread—the grace of God will never reach you." When Hui K'o announces, "I have searched for my mind but can find it nowhere," it sounds almost banal. However, it is a cry of triumph after years of searching in sheer darkness altogether.

The failure a triumph? Hui K'o remarked in one of his talks, "If you are completely one with the purity of the mind-source, then all vows are fulfilled, all practices are completed, all is accomplished. You are no longer subject to states of being. For those who find this body of reality [dharma kaya], the numberless sentient beings are just one good person: the one person who has been there in accord with this through a million billion years." However, you will never find it if you look for it; but if you do not look for it, what hope do you have?

42 The Woman Awakens from Samadhi

*O*nce in ancient times Manjusri went into the presence of the World-Honored One where all the Buddhas assembled, but they had all departed to their original homes. One woman in deepest samadhi sat close to Buddha's throne. Manjusri asked Buddha, "How can this woman be so close to your throne, while I cannot be?" The Buddha replied, "You may awaken this woman yourself and ask her." Manjusri walked around her three times and snapped his fingers once, but could not wake her. He took her up to the Brahman heaven and exerted all his magic powers on her, but still could not awaken her. The World-Honored One said, "Even a hundred thousand Manjusris could not awaken her from her profound samadhi. But deep below, past twelve hundred million lands as innumerable as the sands of the Ganges, lives a Bodhisattva named Momyo. He will be able to awaken this woman. Instantly, Momyo emerged from the earth and bowed to the World-Honored One who told him what he wanted him to do. Momyo went to the woman, snapped his fingers once, and at this she came out of samadhi.

Mumon's Comment

This drama that old Shakya puts on is just a great farce. Tell me now, Manjusri is the teacher of the seven Buddhas, why could he not awaken the woman out of samadhi, while Momyo, a mere beginner, could do so? If without discrimination you can understand the reason for this, then while living a busy, worldly life of affairs you will ever be in dragon samadhi.

Mumon's Verse

> *One could awaken her, the other could not.*
> *Both have their own freedom.*
> *A god-mask, a devil-mask;*
> *The failure was very interesting.*

Comment

This is a koan on which it is becoming increasingly difficult to comment. It is full of subtlety and is quite different from any that we have encountered so far. At the time of the events it records, women were generally considered to be inferior to men and lacking in spirituality. In our age, intelligent people can no longer accept that.

The prejudice against women underlies Manjusri's question, but the koan itself does not harbor this prejudice. On the contrary, at one level, it is showing the folly of it and the cost it has in spiritual development.

Quite apart from this koan, Zen generally is not prejudiced against women. We have already commented on the many stories that tell of women who are in fact superior to men in their understanding and in the depth of their spiritual wisdom. One of these stories, which confirms this point, is the encounter that Sariputra had with the goddess, to which we referred in two earlier koans. Another part of the encounter, which we will relate now, argues against any discrimination being made between men and women in the spiritual life.

Sariputra asks the goddess why she does not transform herself out of her female state. The goddess replies something like Hui K'o in the last koan: "Although I have sought my 'female state' for twelve years, I have not found it." Then she asks Sariputra, "If a magician were to incarnate a woman by magic, would you ask her, 'What prevents you from transforming yourself out of your female state?'" Sariputra replies, "No, because such a woman would not really exist, so there would be nothing to transform." The goddess then uses her magic to switch roles between Sariputra and herself, Sariputra now being the goddess and the goddess, Sariputra. She then says, "Why don't you transform yourself out of the form of a woman?" Sariputra says, "I do not know what to transform." At this the goddess sums up what she has been trying to show: "If Sariputra could again change out of the female state, then all women could change out of their female states. All women appear in the form of women in just the same way that Sariputra appears in the form of a woman. While they are not women in reality, they appear in the form of women." With this in mind, the Buddha said, "In all things, there is neither male nor female."

The koan starts with an enigmatic statement, "Once in ancient times Manjusri went into the presence of the World-Honored One where all the Buddhas assembled, but they had all departed to their original homes." What does this mean? What is it about Manjusri that makes all the Buddhas return to their original home? What, in any case, is the original home of Buddha? Going home is an expression one can use instead of awakening. It is a very good expression because it is down to earth and free of mystique. Imagine you are lost in a forest during a blizzard, with no idea where your home is; in fact, while battling the storm, you may well have forgotten that you even have a home. Your sole concern is to stay alive. Then imagine through good fortune, hard work, and much suffering you finally arrive home. How wonderful it is! How perfect! What a relief! You can let down now, let go all the tension, worry, stress, and fear. You are home. Then what do you do next? Quite likely go across to the fridge, get out a beer, and sink back in an easy chair by the fire. One cannot stay forever starry-eyed on cloud nine.

But does it mean that all the Buddhas go home, and why do they do this even at the approach of Manjusri? Manjusri, Mumon reminds us, was the teacher of Buddhas. What can you teach a Buddha?

Manjusri is also the Bodhisattva of Wisdom. At the Montreal Zen Center at the beginning of sesshin we have a ceremony enshrining Manjusri, who then presides over the entire sesshin. The icon we have is of Manjusri wielding a sword. The sword is held high and is obviously meant to be in motion. Sometimes icons depict Manjusri on a lion. The sword is the sword of prajna, that cuts not in two but in one. In other words, wielding the sword of prajna, Manjusri cuts through the illusion of separation, and discrimination. This is no longer opposed to that, women to men, near to far, awakened to unawakened; all these oppositions melt like ice on a summer's day. The lion represents the courage and invincibility that lies behind wielding the sword of prajna. Furthermore, awakening is sometimes called the lion's roar; if you have heard a lion roar in the wild, and how everything is swallowed up in that one roar, you will have some idea of what is meant.

The koan then describes the woman in deepest samadhi who lay close to Buddha's throne. To be in deep samadhi means to be at one with all. With samadhi the illusion of being a separate individual, a man, a woman, a human being, a self, soul, spirit, I, or whatever, drops away and "Bright and clear shines the moonlight of mind." In samadhi the woman was neither near to nor far from Buddha because Buddha too had "gone home." According to R.H. Blyth, the woman's name was Rii, which literally meant "separated from will or consciousness." In the sleep of ignorance one is separated from will and consciousness, but one is separated from will and consciousness also in samadhi.

Manjusri, however, is looking from the outside and asks why the woman was close to Buddha's throne, but he could not be. In *Verses on the Faith Mind* it is said that the "great Way is not difficult if one makes no judgments," judgments that imply good and bad, superior and inferior, right and wrong. The faith mind is the mind of prajna, and these verses are in praise of prajna, in praise of Manjusri. Manjusri was the teacher of all the Buddhas, and it is in arousing the mind without resting it upon anything, without discrimination, that a Buddha is born. But even so he asks, "How is it that this woman is so close to your throne, and I cannot be?"

Buddha tells Manjusri to awaken the woman from samadhi and ask her himself. But try as he may he cannot waken her. But Buddha knows that far away is Momyo who will be able to awaken her. When Momyo emerged from the earth, he did not question why the woman was near

Buddha, the difference between men and women, what was right and what was wrong, but went to her and snapped his fingers once, and at this she came out of samadhi.

To say, "Deep below, past twelve hundred million countries as innumerable as the sands of the Ganges," is a concrete way of saying that Momyo was as far as it is possible to be from Buddha. Yet one so distant could do what Manjusri was unable to do. Momyo, then, coming from so great a distance, would be what one would call unawakened. However, his name in the sutra from which the koan was originally taken was Rishogai Bosatsu, which according to Blyth, means "throwing off all the shadowy coverings."

In ordinary language, Momyo is the principle of identity, in the same way that Manjusri is the principle of nondifferentiation. That we see the world at all, that we can function in it—drive cars, cook meals, keep accounts, and so on—is due to the work of Momyo. Everything we see is one; but as opposed to the one of nondifferentiation, which is the inclusive one of Manjusri, the one of Momyo is exclusive. In logic, which is the sword of Momyo, a rule says that everything is itself and cannot at the same time be something else, and certainly not its opposite. Without Momyo, nothing would be accomplished, whereas without Manjusri, everything would fall to pieces.

This koan is in a way a mandala. Each of the four protagonists is simultaneously at the center of the action and at a point at the periphery of the action. Each is itself and its opposite. The mandala should be seen to be in motion, like a dance, perhaps like a square dance with partners coming and going. In Zen it is said this very body is the body of Buddha, and this earth where we stand is the pure lotus land. Samsara is Nirvana, Nirvana Samsara. But this word "is" must not be construed as the is of identity but the is of oneness. Manjusri is Momyo, the woman is Buddha, and so on around the square. One end of a stick includes ultimately the other end of the stick; is a snake all head or all tail? If we can see into this we will see, as Mumon warns, "while living a busy, worldly life of affairs you will ever be in dragon samadhi." Dragon samadhi is that samadhi undisturbed by the life of every day.

43 Shuzan's Staff

Shuzan Osho held up a staff in front of his disciples and said, "You monks! If you call this a staff, you hide reality; if you say it is not a staff, you deny the fact. Tell me monks, what will you call it?"

Mumon's Comment

If you call it a staff, you hide reality. If you say it is not a staff, you deny the fact. Don't use words, don't use silence. Now quickly tell me, what is it?

Mumon's Verse

> Holding up the staff,
> He gives life, he takes life.
> Hiding and denying are one whole.
> Even Buddha and patriarchs beg for their lives

Shuzan's Staff

Comment

Gregory Bateson, who coined the expression double bind, uses this koan to illustrate what he means by the term. According to him, a person who is subjected over a period of time to contradictory commands, with the threat of punishment if both are not simultaneously carried out, is faced with a double bind and can develop a psychosis severe enough to cause him to commit suicide.

We have already said that words reveal, but they also hide. Some of the most famous words spoken in this, or any century were $E = MC^2$. These words and the idea that gave them life reveal relationships that were not recognized before, and brought a whole new world into being. Underlying and supporting them was a host of others words or formulas and equations supported and integrated one with the other, like a cathedral made of thought. But for all its beauty and functionality this is still a verbal and thought structure. It is still a veil that transforms the clear light of knowing the way a stained-glass window transforms the light of the sun. In time a new idea and a new word will come into being that will melt down even this elaborate structure and take its place.

But although affirming that words bring worlds into being, Buddhism does not deny the existence of the world. To maintain that the stick is not a stick is to deny what is obvious and before one's face. Philosophy has long struggled with the recognition that although everything seems to be of the mind, one nevertheless cannot deny the world its place. One is reminded of Samuel Johnson's famous refutation of Bishop Berkeley who adhered to the notion that the world was but an idea of God. Johnson slammed his hand on a table, shouting, "Thus do I refute him!" Of course he may only have proved that his hand too was God's idea.

In this realm of thought we cannot refute any extreme. The behaviorist who says that consciousness is an unnecessary postulate, and the idealist who says that the world is but an idea of God, are logically unassailable. It is impossible to prove that being is prior to knowing or knowing prior to being. The war between epistemology and ontology is never ending and always blowing up in new guises. However, Buddha's teaching is neither ontological nor epistemological, although many subsequent commentators have transformed it into one or the other. If one were to use a name for it one would have to say that it is *soteriological* and provisional. In the *Diamond Sutra* Buddha describes his teaching of the good law as, "Likened unto a raft. The dharma must be relinquished; how much more so adharma." In other words, all teaching: the sacred, the dharma, and the profane, the adharma, are provisional. Just as all teaching is provisional, so are all words, fixing as they do a point of view that nevertheless is ever changing. The same thing is a house, if I want to sell it, a home if I am living in it, a building if I am constructing it, property if I am investing in it, and so on. Having said that, we can now say the same thing is neither thing nor the same; and having said that we have now turned the same thing into a philosophical proposition. Don't say it is a thing; don't say it is not a thing. What is it?

> *Holding up the staff,*
> *He gives life, he takes life.*
> *Hiding and denying are one whole.*
> *Even Buddha and patriarchs beg for their lives.*

44 Basho's Staff

*B*asho Osho said to his disciples, "If you have a staff, I will give you one. If you do not have a staff, I will take it from you."

Mumon's Comment

It enables me to wade across a river when the bridge is down. It accompanies me to the village on a moonless night. If you call it a staff, you'll go to hell like an arrow.

Mumon's Verse

The heights and valleys of the world
All are in its grasp.
It supports heaven and sustains the earth.
Everywhere, it manifests the truth.

Comment

This koan seems to be talking about the law of the world.

Those who have get more, those who do not have lose even what they have: the rich get richer and the poor get poorer. However, as we know, a koan does not make statements about social or economic forces, and we have to look deeper to see what is really at issue. On one level Basho's statement echoes the words of Jesus, "Unto them that hath shall be given, unto them that hath not shall be taken even that which they hath."

A Christian saint once said, "If faith, then faith." Faith feeds on itself, and the more faith one has the more one gets. This is so because the more faith one has, the more one can afford to doubt, or, better still, the more one can afford to face one's doubts and the more one can therefore see that the doubts are without substance. Hakuin likens Zen practice to investing. The more one has the more one can invest and eventually the more one has to invest.

He tells the story of two brothers who found a small sum of money that they divided equally. They then parted and each went their way. After a number of years they met again. One brother was harried and care worn, the other radiant and full of life. They compared their use of the money. The first said that he had hoarded the money and protected it from loss, the second that he had thrown it away. When asked by the first brother how he could have done such a thing, the second brother explained that he had bought silk with the money, and from the proceeds had bought hemp, and from that had bought grain, fish, fruit, and meat, and so on. He had invested the money and had had constant returns, so much so he now had more money than he could ever use.

What Hakuin was talking about was obviously awakening. Many who have an initial kensho become obsessed with it, maintaining a special lifestyle, mixing with particular kinds of people, and dressing themselves in a special way, often in the robes of a monk or priest. This is tantamount to hoarding the awakening. On the other hand, another will return directly into life and work within its trials and tribulations without constant reference to "I am awakened" as support. He will encounter difficulty, pain, and anguish, but will not pretend to be other than he is or be troubled why he, an awakened person, meets with these difficulties. He will maintain an inner faith that the truth he sees will eventually triumph because it is real. He feels no need to show others that he is awakened, no need to draw attention to himself in any way at all. Little by little, of itself the truth will shine through. Applying himself constantly to zazen, taking what is given at the moment and working with it, nothing can stop that initial small sum of money becoming a vast fortune that he can freely give to others.

Another deeper interpretation is possible, and Mumon's verse reveals what this koan is really about. "The heights and valleys of the world, are all in its grasp." Again a quotation from Jesus will help: "What does it matter if you have the whole world and lose your soul in the process?" To have the whole world and not have it that supports the whole world is to have nothing. Not to have that which has the heights and valleys of the world in its grasp is to gain the world and lose your soul. "If you have a staff," says Unmon, "I will give you one." In terms of practice one can have the world of buildings, temples, patronage, and large membership; one can have ritual and ceremony, robes, transmissions, the correct posture and technique. But without it of what use is all this? If you say you have a stick, I'll give you one.

On the other hand, if you do not have a stick I will take it away from you. Someone asked Joshu, "If there is nothing at all, what then?" Joshu replied, "Throw it out." "And if there is nothing to throw out?" "Then carry it out," said Joshu.

In "East Coker," T. S. Eliot, quoting St. John of the Cross, said:

> *In order to arrive at what you do not know*
> *You must go by a way which is the way of ignorance.*
> *In order to possess what you do not possess*
> *You must go by the way of dispossession.*
> *In order to arrive at what you are not*
> *You must go through the way in which you are not.*[13]

But we must not cling to this not knowing, not having.

If you have it you lose all. Clinging to not knowing, clinging to a dead void, staying in dead emptiness is the danger that threatens the one who has had the temerity to question everything and to see with a clear eye that from the beginning not a thing is. Hakuin's teacher called him a devil in the hole, a wonderful description of one lost in emptiness, clinging to it.

It is not an empty abstraction with no connection with my life. For the Westerner who even objects to walking across a parking lot, it is difficult to perceive the importance of the staff to the monk. But for people used to walking long distances across terrain without even a path, a staff would have been a familiar friend. "It enables me to cross the river when the bridge is down," says Mumon. But it would also have served as a companion and a protector when "It accompanies me to the village on a moonless

---

13 *The Four Quartets.* T. S. Eliot. (London: Faber and Faber, 1944).

night." One is reminded again of the Christian tradition, this time of the Twenty-third Psalm:

> *Yea though I walk through the valley of the shadow of*
>   *death,*
> *I will fear no evil; for thou art with me:*
> *Thy rod and thy staff they comfort me.*

Mumon says,

> *The heights and valleys of the world*
> *All are in its grasp.*
> *It supports heaven and sustains the earth.*
> *Everywhere, it manifests the truth.*

It manifests the truth everywhere because, as someone said, "The Lord is in my eye, that is why I see him everywhere."

45 Hoen's "Who is He?"

H oen of Tozan said, "Even Shakya and Maitreya are his servants. Who is he?"

Mumon's Comment

If you can truly recognize him with perfect clarity, it is like meeting your own father at the crossroads. You do not need to ask another if it is he or not.

Mumon's Verse

> Don't draw another's bow,
> Don't ride another's horse,
> Don't discuss another's faults,
> Don't meddle in another's affairs.

Comment

Maitreya is the future Buddha; so this koan says that past and future Buddhas are his servants, and then asks, "Who is he?" In our culture some might say the Trinity: God the Father, God the Son, and God the Holy Ghost are his servants; who is he? Someone asked Joshu, "Who is the one that transcends even Buddha?" And Joshu replied, "That man leading his oxen, it is he."

In Japanese Buddhism two ways are available—the way of *self*-power and the way of *other* power. The Pure Land school, in which one throws oneself onto the mercy and grace of Amitabha Buddha, is an example of other power. I can do nothing, all must be accomplished by the power of the other. The Christian way, which generally speaking is the way of the other power, can be summed up in a line from the Lord's Prayer, "Thy will be done." The most common example of self-power is Zen. Although useful to some degree, this kind of generalization can lead to considerable misunderstanding if we consider the I or self and thou to be two substances, with I over here and thee over there, and an unbridgeable abyss between. In the Pure Land this misunderstanding can lead to obsequiousness, a reduction of oneself to nullity. In the Zen school it can lead to a particular kind of arrogance, a spiritual strutting.

I and thou are but two poles of that which has no definition, no boundary. In the full encounter with Shakya, with Maitreya, no thing is *encountered*, but by this we must not sink into the pit of solipsism. Martin Buber put this well: "When *Thou* is spoken, the speaker has no thing for his object. For when there is a thing there is another thing. Every It is bounded by others; It exists only through being bounded by others. But when *Thou* is spoken there is no thing. *Thou* has no grounds." But on another occasion, "What then do we experience of Thou? Just nothing. For we do not experience it. What then do we know of Thou? Just everything. *For we know nothing isolated about it any more.*[14]

Buber emphasizes that the relation to the thou is direct. "No system of ideas, no foreknowledge and no fancy intervene between I and Thou. The memory itself is transformed as it plunges out of its isolation into the unity of the whole." Here we have the way that Buddha and Maitreya are his servants. Without them he would simply be bound in his own knowing. The Sufi mystic says of God, "I was a hidden treasure and yearned to be known. Then I created creatures in order to be known by them." We create God in our own image because God has created us in his. Buber observed, "God is the wholly other; but He is also the wholly Same, the wholly Present . . . nearer to me than my I." To know this, "No aim, no lust and no anticipation [can] intervene between I and Thou. Every means is an obstacle. Only when every means has collapsed does the meeting come about." Furthermore, no way is available but "He who goes out with his whole being to meet his Thou and carries to it all being that is in the world, finds Him who cannot be sought." It is under these conditions that you can, as Mumon declared, "truly recognize him with perfect clarity, it is like meeting your own father at the crossroads. You do not need to ask another if it is he or not."

---

[14] From *I and Thou* by Martin Buber.

46 Take a Step from the Top of a Hundred-Foot Pole

*S*ekiso Osho asked, *"How will you step from the top of a hundred-foot pole?"* Another eminent master of old said, *"You, who sit on the top of a hundred-foot pole, although you have come to realization you are not yet real. Go forward from the top of the pole and you will manifest your whole body in the ten directions."*

Mumon's Comment

If you go on and turn your body about, nowhere are you not the master. But even so, tell me, how will you take a step from the top of a hundred-foot pole?

Mumon's Verse

> *Blinding the eye of insight,*
> *Clinging to the mark on the scale.*
> *Even though he may sacrifice his life,*
> *He is only a blind man leading the blind.*

Comment

It seems the master saw some acrobats who were climbing to the top of a pole. The master turned to his disciple with a question: "They can only get to the top of a hundred-foot pole. How would you go beyond that? How would you take another step?" The distinguishing mark of Buddha's teaching is in exhorting one to take that next step. When he left home, Buddha met several teachers, each of whom took him a little deeper into the way of samadhi. Each took him a little higher, even to the summit of a hundred-foot pole. But Buddha turned his back on this teaching, saying it can in no way bring a final resolution of the deep anguish of life and death.

A great temptation lies in spiritual training to leave behind the world of suffering and to seek a world of unity and peace. This is tantamount to getting to the top of a hundred-foot pole. It is of little value and can only end in the person sliding down again into the darkness and obscurity that await him below. Such a person is clinging to the appearance while ignoring the fact. It is like one who takes the reading of the scale for the weight of the thing. No matter the sacrifices that he may have made, such a person, because the eye of wisdom is closed, will be like the blind leading the blind.

But how to make the leap?

This same challenge awaits us at every crossroad of our lives. Time and again we find ourselves in a cul-de-sac, unable to go forward, unable to retreat, unable to stay where we are, and unable to make up our minds what to do. We hesitate and prevaricate, put things off until tomorrow, wish things were different, and curse fate for making us choose. But still we are stuck. People who are on the Way often encounter a cul-de-sac in practice and experience great dread and panic. It is a feeling of having done something that can never be undone, without any idea of what it might be or its consequences. It is a kind of spiritual vertigo.

A master who heard of this koan said, "On top of a hundred-foot pole an iron cow gives birth to a calf." How often it happens at the darkest moment, and from a direction totally unexpected, a light breaks through. But only when we have finally made up our minds to leap does the new birth take place. One person who had attended a retreat was on his way home and had to cross a railway line. Just as he was crossing a train sounded its whistle and the man came to awakening.

To get all we must give all. A story is told of a woman who was a follower of Gurdjieff. She was wealthy and very much attached to her wealth. Gurdjieff told her if she wanted to continue working with him she would have to give him all her jewelry. She was shocked by this and did not know what to do. One moment she was sure he was a charlatan and simply wanted to steal her wealth. The next she thought of how precious his teaching was, how much it meant to her life, and how impossible it would be to live without it. Then she remembered how much she loved her jewels and how cruel it was to ask her to surrender them. But she admitted to herself how useless they really were, as she had very little opportunity to wear them yet had the responsibility of looking after them, keeping them insured, and so on. Around and around she went, unable to sleep, unable to come to a decision. She thought of asking Gurdjieff to withdraw his demand, but realized at some level it was a necessary sacrifice she had to make. Eventually she made the decision. She put all the jewels in a box, took the box, and, in tears, gave it to Gurdjieff. Gurdjieff took one look inside and thrust the box back, saying, "It is no longer necessary for you to give me these."

We desperately want to know something, and so seek to know peace, serenity, and joy. The great danger of the first kensho, which is invariably seeing into emptiness, is that we can stop there wanting to treasure the joy and serenity revealed to us. But, as Unmon once warned, even a good thing is not as good as nothing. To know is enough, to know something is far too much, even if at some subtle level it is knowing nothing. To know anything, even if it is as small as a speck of dust, is to obscure it all. But once we know, the whole world manifests who we are, and nothing can get in the way. The step forward is a clear light.

47 Tosotsu's Three Barriers

*T*osotsu's Etsu Osho set up three barriers for his disciples:

You leave no stone unturned to explore profundity, simply to see into your true nature. Now, I want to ask you, right at this moment, where is your true nature?

If you realize your true nature, you are free from life and death. Tell me, when your eyesight dims in the final moments, how can you be free from life and death?

When you free yourself from life and death, you should know where you are going. So when the four elements disintegrate, where will you go?

Mumon's Comment

If you can give a turning word to these three questions, you are the master wherever you may stand, and command Zen whatever circumstances you are in. If not, listen: gulping down your meal will fill you easily, but chewing it will sustain you.

Mumon's Verse

> *In one moment is eternity;*
> *Eternity is just this moment.*
> *If you see through this moment's moment,*
> *You see through the one who sees through this*
> *moment.*

Comment

Oddly enough, in the tradition in which I did my training, one has to pass these koans before one can start working on the rest of the *Mumonkan.* I say oddly enough, because they are, in a way, among the most penetrating of all the koans in the *Mumonkan.*

   The monks to whom Tosotsu would have been talking had most likely traveled around from monastery to monastery, from teacher to teacher, always searching for true nature. Nowadays in the West the pure waters of Zen are being muddied, and more and more it is said that Buddha and the patriarchs did not really mean one should search for one's true nature. Some say the essence of the Way is in living an ethical life, others advocate just sitting in meditation and forcing oneself to take up the lotus posture even at risk of knees and ankles. Others prefer to read books and attend conferences. But the word Buddha means *awakened.* To be awakened is to be awakened in, and therefore to, true nature. Zen teachers who teach anything less than this are cheating their students. But true nature can only be found after an exhaustive search, after one has used up all one's resources. At that moment, when one searches but has no idea of how, why, or even if the search can be continued, where is your true nature?

   Without awakening, kensho, satori, paravritti, call it

what you will, Buddhism has very little to offer the West except more abstruse philosophy and an ethical system in no way superior to the Christian. What Buddha taught had more or less been taught by the Vedanta. He added little. It was not in his teaching that Buddha was Buddha, but in his awakening. After that, everything he said was significant. It is said that in the mouths of fools even the words of the wise are foolish. But in the mouths of the wise, the words of fools are true.

To practice Buddhism, as Dogen said, is to know the self; to know the self is to forget the self and to forget the self is to be one with the ten thousand things. All of this is but an elaborate and direct way of talking about kensho, satori, or awakening. All kinds of reasons are nowadays given why this knowing the self, advocated by Dogen, is not possible: it is too difficult, it is not possible for modern Westerners, it is not possible for lay people, and so on. Every one of these reasons is but an excuse. They simply come from the mouths of the modern-day scribes and Pharisees. And the words of Jesus are still apt: "Woe to you scribes and Pharisees, hypocrites! because you shut the kingdom of heaven against men: for you enter not in yourselves, neither suffer ye them that are entering in to enter."

Tosotsu continues, "If you realize your true nature, you are free from life and death." It is this that all the great religions in their own way have promised. In Christianity it is life eternal, in Zen Buddhism freedom from birth and death. *But one must realize one's true nature.* Tosotsu tells his monks, "You leave no stone unturned to explore profundity, simply to see into your true nature." To leave no stone unturned. To give oneself over entirely to the quest, to the search. "Now," says Tosotsu, "I want to ask you, right at this moment, where is your true nature?" "Seek ye first the kingdom of heaven and all things will be added unto you." But in the very moment of search, where is true nature, where is the kingdom of heaven?

Then Tosotsu asks the question that humankind has been asking since the dawn of time, frequently in the middle of the night under a crushing burden of fear and nausea. "Tell me, when your eyesight dims in the final moments, how can you be free from life and death?" He promises, "If you realize your true nature, you are free from life and death." Who would not want such freedom? What price would one not pay, what burden would one not bear if we could be guaranteed the certainty that this is true. What is death?

Most people, when they struggle with fear about death, have three things confused in their minds. Most are concerned about the suffering that so often accompanies dying. Most are also concerned about dying itself: leaving loved ones, leaving unfinished work, leaving the beauty of life. Third is the fear of death.

It is this fear of death that we address in our practice. With a steadfast mind one dwells hardly at all on the suffering that accompanies death or the dying process. But facing up to it is what practice is all about. It is said that if you die before you die, you do not die when you die. A monk went to a master and announced, "I am not afraid of death." The master remarked, "Oh, bad luck." Without that fear, where will we get the energy to die before we die?

The thought of the death of the body, of the loss of all sensation, is painful, but the thought of the loss of I is terrifying. One thing we must always bear in mind: we know nothing of our own death. We may see a thousand people die but we still know nothing of our own death. This means whatever fear we have is not the fear of death, *but fear of the idea of death.*

I is always dying. Every new moment brings forth a new I. The discovery of the phenomenon of multiple personalities only confirms what we have in our hearts always known: we are not just one individual but a multitude. Each one of this multitude reflects in its own way the original one. The life of birth and death is the life of the constant coming and going of the reflections. The moon on the waves, now scattered, now unified.

To realize oneself is to turn away from the fascination of the reflection and find this one; this moon is real, is indeed the only reality. Turning away from the fascination of the reflection is the death before we die, because of which we do not die when we die. This one is never absent: even in our search for it, it is present. Narcissus fell in love with his own reflection in a pool and, trying to embrace it, fell in and drowned. The body supports the mirror, this mirror, which has a thousand facets, is the personality. If one morning you were looking at yourself in the bathroom mirror and someone threw a brick and destroyed the mirror, what would become of you? "If you realize your true nature, you are free from life and death." Every drop of dew in the morning reflects the sun. As the sun mounts in the sky the drops dry up, but the sun shines on even though unreflected.

Tosotsu asks, "When you set yourself free from life and death, you should know where you are going. So when the four elements separate, where will you go?" Don't wait for the four elements to separate; where are you right now? Where you are right now is where you will go. Ramana Maharshi said, at his death, "I am not going anywhere, there is nowhere to go." Where is that nowhere? Where does that question go when it is no longer thought?

48 Kempo's One Road

A monk said to Kempo, "It is written, 'Bhaga-vats in the ten directions. One road to Nirvana.' I still wonder where that road can be." Kempo lifted his staff and drew a line, saying, "Here it is."

Later a monk asked the same question of Ummon, who held up his fan and replied, "This fan jumps up to the thirty-third heaven and hits the nose of the deity Saka Dvanam Indra. When you strike the carp of the eastern sea, the rain pours down in torrents."

Mumon's Comment

One, going to the bottom of the sea, lifts up clouds of dust; the other, on top of the highest mountain, raises towering waves to wash the sky. One holding fast, the other letting go—each stretches out his hand to support the deepest teaching. They are just like two little boys running from opposite ends and colliding with each other. But no one can be absolutely direct. When examined with a true eye, neither of these masters knows the road.

Koans: Forty-eight

Mumon's Verse

> *Before a step is taken, the goal is reached;*
> *Before the tongue has moved, the speech is finished.*
> *Though each move is ahead of the next,*
> *There is still a transcendent secret.*

Comment

Where is the road to Nirvana? Many people who come to workshops ask, "What exactly is Zen? How does one really practice?" One of the things we do on the beginners' course is give simple exercises to help people be present during the week. Sometimes people wonder, "What do you mean, be present?" One cannot say presence is nowhere nor everywhere, both are abstract and simply ways of talking. But to say presence, or coming to awakening, is doing this or that is no good either. To say, for example, only by the practice of Buddhism, or Zen Buddhism, or Rinzai Zen Buddhism can one come to awakening is to reduce what is a common heritage of all humankind to some parochial, system-bound technique. To say one can reach salvation only through the Church is similarly like trying to put the sky in a zoo. These all limit the truth to some system or other, to some set of beliefs or theories.

One day I met a woman on the train who at one time had been a member of the Montreal Zen Center. We spent some time talking, and during the course of the conversation she told me she was now working with another teacher, well known in North America. She described his retreats, during which a lot of time was spent walking about "being present." "He tells us that we must be constantly aware; when we pick up a cup, we must feel the cup, feel its smoothness, its roundness, its weight. It is like this with all the other senses. We must really see, really hear." I asked, "Do you like this teaching?" "Oh yes!" she enthused. "At last I know what I am supposed to do. He has given me something concrete. With you everything was always so vague." I wonder what she would have thought of Kempo's response, or Unmon's?

On another occasion a man asked me a question and then admonished, "Please don't give some clever Zen answer." The implication was one should be able to answer any question in a straightforward manner, but, being "a Zen Buddhist," I preferred to wrap the answer up in enigmas. However, both Kempo and Unmon are responding in as straightforward a manner as they know how. We must have faith to tackle a koan: Zen masters are not trying to be obscure, they are replying as clearly and as directly as they can. If we do not have this faith, if we think that a koan is deliberately misleading us or using some code, or kicking sand in our eyes, we will try to break the code, or find a better, more outright way of saying what the koan is saying in its circumlocution.

However, we do sometimes need the terms of the koan explained as they may refer to sutras or other aspects of Buddhism that we are not familiar with. Thus, for example, the expression, "bhagavats in the ten directions," means throughout everywhere. Everywhere you look are Buddhas. Everywhere you look are saviors. Yet *one Way only* lies open to Nirvana. It is not the way of Zen or Sufism, or the inner glance or anything else like this. So what is it?

Another way of understanding "bhagavats in the ten directions" is that it means you are already whole and complete, you are fully awakened. Only one way exists by which you can know this. The monk wondered, "What is this one

Way?" In reply Kempo drew a line with his stick and said, "It is here." Where did Kempo draw the line? Not on empty space, or nowhere. In Zen it is said, "It is right before your face." But don't let us be content with this reply. Ask again, where did Kempo draw the line?

To help see into this reply of Kempo, Mumon tells us about Unmon's response, which is at the other end of the world entirely. With Unmon, the highest of all possible heavens is within reach of his fan; with just one flick it hits the nose of the deity there. Unmon also says, "When you strike the carp of the eastern sea, the rain pours down in torrents." Action, action, action, pure dynamic action. Mumon picks up this action, this sheer energy: "One, going to the bottom of the sea, lifts up clouds of dust; the other, on top of the highest mountain, raises towering waves to wash the sky." How do you raise dust at the bottom of the sea? How do you have waves washing the sky? Limits, the opposites, are lost in the one Way. Kempo has the essence, Unmon the function, both have the one Way. So now, what is the one Way to what you already are?

Mumon's Postscript

The sayings and doings of the Buddha and the patriarchs have been set down in their original form. Like the confessions of a criminal they have all been set down. Nothing extra has been added by the author who has taken the lid off his head and showed his eyeballs. Realize it directly; do not go outside. If you are an awakened one you will immediately get the point at the merest indication of it. You have to pass through no gate; no steps have to be ascended. Go through the check point, with your head up, without seeking permission of the gatekeeper.

Do you not remember Gensha's saying, "No-gate is the gate of liberation, no-mind is the mind of the one on the Way." And Hakuun says, "The way is clear before you; it is just this! Go through!"

However, all of this kind of talk is like mixing milk and mud. If you have passed the Gate without a door, you can make a fool of Mumon. If not, you are deceiving yourself. It is easy to know the mind of emptiness but the wisdom of differentiation is difficult to attain. When you do realize such wisdom then the world will be naturally at peace.

Respectfully inscribed by Mumon Ekai Bhikkhu,
eighth in succession from Yogi

Mumon's Warnings

To stick to the regulations and keep to the rules is tying
oneself without a rope.
To do what you like in every sitution is mindless and
selfish.

To recognize mind and purify it is the false Zen of silent
illumination.
To go off and do your thing is to fall into a deep pit.

To be be absolutely present and clear all the time is to
wear chains and an iron yoke.
To be lost in good and evil belongs to heaven and hell.
Looking for Buddha and the Dharma is to be confined in
two iron mountains.

He who realizes it as soon as a thought arises is one who
exhausts his energies.
To sit blankly in quietism is the practice of the dead.

If one makes progress, one fools oneself.
If one retreats, one betrays the dharma.
If one neither progresses nor retreats, one is simply a
warm corpse.

Now tell me, what will you do? You must make the utmost
effort to come to awakening in this life, lest you have
eternal regret.

Appendix One

Excerpts from the *Diamond Sutra*

One day, at breakfast time, the World-Honored One put on his robe and carrying his bowl made his way into the great city of Shravasti to beg for his food. In the midst of the city he begged from door to door according to the rule. This done he returned to his retreat and ate his meal. When he had finished he put away his robe and begging bowl, washed his feet, arranged his seat, and sat down.

Subhuti asked:

World-Honored One, if good men and good women seek the consummation of incomparable awakening, by what standards of judgment should they abide and how should they control their thoughts?

Buddha said:

I will tell you what these standards of judgment are. Bodhisattvas should discipline their thoughts thus:

All living beings are caused by me to attain unbounded liberation Nirvana. Yet when vast innumerable, immeasurable numbers of beings have been liberated not one being has been liberated. Why is this? It is because no Bodhisattva who is a real Bodhisattva cherishes the idea of an ego-entity, a personality, a being, or a separated individuality.

Furthermore, in the practice of charity a Bodhisattva should be detached. That is to say he should practice charity without regard to appearance.

Is the Tathagata to be recognized by some material characteristic?

No, World-Honored One; the Tathagata cannot be recognized by any material characteristic. Wherefore?

Because the Tathagata has said that material characteristics are not in fact material characteristics.

Wheresoever there are material characteristics there is delusion; but who so perceives that all characteristics are in fact no-characteristics perceives the Tathagata.

My teaching of the good law is to be likened unto a raft. The dharma must be relinquished; how much more so adharma.

Has the Tathagata attained the consummation of incomparable enlightenment?

Has the Tathagata a teaching to enunciate?

Subhuti answered: As I understand Buddha's meaning there is no formulation of truth called consummation of incomparable enlightenment. Moreover, the Tathagata has no formulated teaching to enunciate. Wherefore? Because the Tathagata has said that truth is uncontainable and inexpressible. It neither is nor is it not.

If anyone receive and retain even four lines of this discourse and explained them to others, his merit would be greater than someone who filled three thousand galaxies of the worlds with seven treasures and gave all away as gifts of alms.

From this discourse issue forth all Buddhas and the consummation of incomparable enlightenment teachings of all Buddhas.

Subhuti said, World-Honored One, when the Buddha declares that I excel amongst holy men in the yoga of perfect quiescence, in dwelling in seclusion, and in freedom from passions, I do not say within myself: I am a holy one of perfect enlightenment free from passions. World-Honored One, if I said within myself: Such am I; you would not declare: Subhuti finds happiness abiding in peace, in seclusion in the midst of the forest. This is because Subhuti abides nowhere therefore he is called Subhuti, Joyful-Abider-in-Peace, Dweller-in-Seclusion-in-the-Forest.

Therefore Subhuti, the Bodhisattva, the great being, should produce a thought of utmost, right, and perfect enlightenment. Unsupported by form should a thought be produced, unsupported by sounds, smells, tastes, touchables, or mind objects should a thought be produced, unsupported by dharmas should a thought be produced, unsupported by anything should a thought be produced. A Bodhisattva should *arouse the mind without resting it upon anything.*

Subhuti, what do you think, has the Tathagata a teaching to enunciate?

World-Honored One, the Tathagata has nothing to teach.

The Tathagata declares that a world is not really a world; it is called "a world."

If anyone listens to this discourse in faith with a pure lucid mind she will thereupon conceive an idea of fundamental reality. We should know that such a one establishes the most remarkable virtue. World-Honored One, such an idea of fundamental reality is not, in fact, a distinctive idea; therefore the Tathagata teaches: "idea of fundamental reality" is merely a name.

Just as you say! If anyone listens to this discourse and is neither filled with alarm nor awe nor dread, be it known that such a one is of remarkable achievement.

No wisdom can we get hold of, no highest perfection,
No Bodhisattva, no Bodhicitta either.
When told of this, if not bewildered and in no way
　anxious,

Appendix One

A Bodhisattva courses in the *Prajnaparamita*.
In form, in feeling, will, perception, and consciousness
Nowhere in them they find a place to rest on.

The mind should be kept independent of any thoughts which arise within it. If the mind depends upon anything whatsoever it has no sure haven. This is why Buddha teaches that the mind of a Bodhisattva should not accept the appearances of things as a basis when exercising charity. As Bodhisattvas practice charity for the welfare of all living beings, they should do so in this manner. Just as the Tathagata declares that all characteristics are no characteristics, so he declares that all living beings are not in fact living beings.

If a Bodhisattva practices charity with a mind attached to formal notions he is like unto a person groping sightless in the gloom; but a Bodhisattva who practices charity with mind detached from any formal notions is like a person with open eyes in the radiant glory of the morning to whom all kinds of objects are clearly visible.

Furthermore, if it be that good men and good women who receive and retain this discourse are downtrodden, their evil destiny is the inevitable retributive result of sins committed in their past mortal lives. By virtue of their present misfortunes the reacting effect of their past will be thereby worked out and they will be in a position to attain the consummation of incomparable enlightenment.

One who is reviled by others has transgressed in former lives, which doom him or her to fall into evil worlds; but because of the scorn and vilification by others in the present lifetime the transgressions in the former life are wiped out.

It is impossible to retain past mind, impossible to hold on to present mind, and impossible to grasp future mind.

Do not say that the Tathagata conceives the idea; I must set forth a teaching. For if anyone says that the Tathagata sets forth a teaching, he really slanders Buddha and is unable to explain what I teach.

Through the consummation of incomparable enlightenment I acquired not the least thing; wherefore it is called "consummation of incomparable enlightenment."

Though the common people accept egoity as real, the Tathagata declares that ego is not different from non-ego. Whom the Tathagata referred to as common people are not really common people such is merely a name.

Who sees me by form,
Who seeks me in sound,
Perverted are his footsteps upon the way;
For he cannot perceive the Tathagata.

If anyone should say that the Tathagata comes or goes or sits or reclines he fails to understand my teaching, because Tathagata has neither whence nor whither, therefore is he called Tathagata.

Words cannot explain the real nature of a cosmos. Only common people fettered with desire make use of this arbitrary method.

Thus shall you think of all this fleeting world
A star at dawn, a bubble in a stream;
A flash of lightning in a summer cloud,
A flickering lamp, a phantom and a dream.

Appendix Two

Prajnaparamita Hridaya
"Heart of Perfect Wisdom"

This translation was done by the Rochester Zen Center and is reproduced with their permission. It is the version used by that center and by the Montreal Zen Center for chanting.

The Bodhisattva of Compassion, from the depths of Prajna
    wisdom,
saw the emptiness of all five skandhas
and sundered the bonds of suffering.
Know then: Form here is only emptiness, emptiness only
    form
Form is no other than emptiness,
Emptiness no other than form.
Feeling, thought and choice, consciousness itself,
are the same as this.
Dharmas here are empty, all are the primal void.
None are born or die,
Nor are they stained or pure, nor do they wax or wane.
So in emptiness no form, no feeling, thought or choice,
Nor is there consciousness.
No eye, ear, nose, tongue, body, mind;
no color, sound, smell, taste, touch, or what the mind takes
    hold of,
nor even act of sensing.
No ignorance or end of it, nor all that comes of ignorance:
no withering, no death, no end of them.
Nor is there pain, or cause of pain, or cease in pain,

or noble path to lead from pain.
Not even wisdom to attain, attainment too is emptiness.
So know that the Bodhisattva, holding to nothing whatever,
But dwelling in prajna wisdom, is freed of delusive hin-
    drance,
rid of the fear bred by it, and reaches clearest nirvana.
All buddhas of past and present, buddhas of future time,
through faith in prajna wisdom come to full enlightenment.
Know then the great dharani, the radiant peerless mantra,
the supreme, unfailing mantra, the *Prajnaparamita,*
whose words allay all pain.
This is highest wisdom, true beyond all doubt,
know and proclaim its truth:

Gate, gate, Paragate, Parasamgate, bodhi, sva-ha!

Appendix Three

An Account of Awakening

Lighting a Lamp of the Law

The following is an account of kensho that I wrote at the request of Roshi Philip Kapleau after a rohatsu sesshin in December 1974. It is taken from *Zen Bow* (winter and spring 1975, published by the Rochester Zen Center, Rochester, New York) and is reproduced by their permission. It was written in the hope that it might inspire others on the long and somewhat lonely journey of awakening, and is reprinted for that reason as well as to give an example of what it means to work on the koan Mu!

Zen Bow editor's note: This article began as a letter to roshi from a 45-year-old man, capsuling his post-sesshin experience. After reading it, we urged him to write at greater length about his daily life and practice. Excerpts from this account comprise the first section of the article. He was also asked to describe more fully his experience at the sesshin, leading up to kensho. Following this comes the actual letter to roshi, an afterword, and a response by the roshi. It is hoped that the article will not only be interesting to *Zen Bow* readers, but will also be a source of encouragement and inspiration to our practice.

Daily Practice

My work is in the personnel department of a company and consists in administering salaries and doing organization analysis. According to the way people judge these things, it could be said that I am moderately successful and probably in line for promotion to a vice-presidential position in the not too distant future.

My marriage has been a great success and has produced three very fine children. My life is a full one with varied interests.

This is all said because so often people worry about whether they can possibly carry on Zen practice and live in the world at the same time. But really they should not be concerned because it is entirely possible. It is unlikely that anyone would consider me exceptional, and it should be taken as a great consolation that if one person can carry on Zen practice, a full business career, and family life, anyone can do it.

However, it is not done without what one might call sacrifice, nor without determination and some measure of courage. Perhaps this story might help others to arouse this determination in themselves.

I started real Zen practice in 1966 when, through a series of coincidences or good karma, I encountered Yasutani Roshi. He had the kindness to visit Canada and conduct a zazenkai or workshop for eleven most unlikely candidates for Buddhism. Before this encounter my spiritual life had been one flounder after another, until in 1964, exhausted and depressed, I started sitting. This "sitting" was completely untutored and could not strictly be called Zen, but it did give some results. The value of a teacher was apparent to me once I met with Yasutani, and he showed me the correct postures to use for meditation, how to follow the breath and so on.

After the zazenkai I made inquiries about further Zen training. Can anyone imagine the joy and gratitude that was felt on hearing that a sesshin was about to take place in

Rochester, at which an American Zen teacher, Philip Kapleau, was to be installed?

But the joy also had a most devastating effect on me in that it awakened in some way the most terrible fear of death, which was to haunt me almost without respite for the next two years. My blood pressure rose alarmingly, and I was saturated by terrible anxiety and psychological numbness. I was terrified of being alone, and as my work necessitated frequent visits away from home and staying overnight in hotels, I sometimes felt like a being in hell. On one occasion I was so sure that I was going to die that I stopped the car and got out so that I would not die unattended. As it happened, the shock of the cold air when getting out of the car braced me and brought me back to my senses.

The doctor recommended tranquilizers, but I knew that to yield to these would probably be the end of zazen. In any case, there was the constant and abiding faith that zazen would of itself, in due time, bring about a cure. During this period, my teacher gave constant encouragement and pointed out that, in effect, to have such a fear was good fortune in that it would drive one deeper into one's practice, as indeed it turned out to do. The force and power of the anxiety aroused great energy and the sitting that was done during those anxious times was very deep.

My work was also a great help and, although I was constantly tempted to withdraw from it in some way, I hung on. The very mundaneness, the inconsequential problems, the battles and disagreements, gave support that enabled me to continue my practice. Although the struggle was wearing, in a deep way a profound reconciliation developed between my life of Zen and my business life. More and more they ceased to be two independent lives. The constant humiliations that were suffered through trying to introduce new ideas (and these humiliations sometimes were very great) were a powerful ego abrasive. Thomas Merton tells the story of a Christian monk who paid people to humiliate him, and many Zen stories tell of masters who humiliate their most ardent followers because they know that humiliation undoubtedly is the greatest ally that a person who is serious in his practice can have. It truly has no parallel. Used wisely and without cowering, it corrodes the ego like acid.

During one hot summer I developed insomnia. It started through my losing one or two nights' sleep because of the heat and then my becoming concerned that the sitting schedule that I had established so painfully would be upset. This insomnia was to last for eighteen months, during which time I suffered some of the most excruciating tensions. Once again there was no question of taking sleeping pills. I tried them once or twice, but they ruined the sitting for the next day. Sometimes it was possible to sit instead of sleep, but at other times the tension became so great that I could do nothing but crawl around the room on my hands and knees. It is said that religion begins with a cry for help, and there have been several times when silently I cried out with all my force, "Oh you forces of good in the universe, please, please come to my help now!" Strangely enough, when this cry came from the hara, the very pit of the stomach, there would be peace. My teacher urged me to go on with zazen. "Go to work exhausted if you have to, but don't give up your practice."

Of course, there is the problem of time. One does have to practice intensely and it is also necessary to give a good deal of time to it. My wife and I have practiced zazen now for eight years from 5:00 until 7:20 each morning. This means that we have to rise about 4:30 a.m. daily, with a rest on Saturday morning. We also practice for an hour in the evening, again with Friday evening off when we sometimes go to a show. Once a month, except during the very hot weather, the two of us have a one- or two-day sitting over a weekend. We also found it helpful to read inspirational books, particularly those telling of accounts of monks and laymen who have overcome difficulties in their search for enlightenment. So, in effect, much of our time is spent in Buddhism.

The Rohatsu Sesshin

In a way the Rohatsu sesshin, the one that commemorates the Buddha's great awakening, started in October. At that sesshin a new hope was generated. This hope, with the abiding faith that has stayed with me, gave me the conviction that success would be mine. Between October and December my wife and I spent our time preparing for the sesshin. We sat through several weekends, attended Jukai at the Toronto Zen Center, and had a "word fast" in which we read and wrote as little as possible. When Rohatsu came around we were both well prepared, so much so that when talking to one of the monitors I proclaimed, "This is my sesshin." This came up from the hara with unnatural force and I felt foolish. To my surprise I found that I was weeping.

The Rohatsu sesshin, at which about fifty of us were attending, lasted seven days and was held as usual at the Rochester Zen Center. Most, if not all, were seasoned practicers as this was a very rigorous sesshin. The first two days proceeded without incident. The normal settling-in was done. On the third day the roshi tested me and I was aware

of the spontaneity of the responses and of his evident pleasure. I yelled at the top of my voice and pounded the floor,
"This is my sesshin!"

Returning to the zendo I flung myself totally into the
koan. At a point at which I was almost one with the koan,
one of the monitors tapped me on the shoulder and told me
to go to dokusan (the private interview with the roshi). I
was surprised, because I had already been to dokusan, and
the roshi did not encourage participants to go to it twice in
one dokusan period. I tried to explain to the monitor with
gestures but, with a Fudo-like expression and an unanswer-
able pointing finger, he ordered me to dokusan. I went.

Once again the roshi questioned and answers came.
This was indeed my sesshin.

The next few days were an unmitigated fury. Urged on
by the kyosaku (the stick used to encourage one to greater
efforts), the shouts of the monitors, and the roshi, I tried to
get deeper into my koan, but thoughts always persisted. Try
as I might during the work period, my mind wandered.
During mealtime, despite constant warnings, my mind
slipped constantly to food rather than to the koan.

The hope that had been nurtured by the two months
between sesshins slipped away. The old doubts crept in: I
can never do this; all of those who have passed their first
koan are on the staff; they are all young and can take it;
look at so-and-so, how hard he has worked, and he is not
through his koan. What chance is there for me? The taut-
ness of the mind slackened. It was hopeless, and with that,
despair rose up.

For a brief moment I let go of the koan and reasoned
thus. I feel such hopelessness because I yearn for mu so
much. If there were not such a tremendous need for mu,

there would not be this discouragement or despair. In fact then, despair is my ally—it is the measure and expression of my need. I could therefore despair, and despair at my despair, because that very despair was on my side. "Your true nature is trying to come into consciousness." My teacher had said this so often. This despair was the voice of my true nature! This all passed through the mind in a flash, but having seen this my heart opened up and a great yearning for mu took possession of me.

I yearned for mu so much that my own body was not enough for the task, and I borrowed, as it were, the bodies of all the sesshin participants, of the monitors, of the roshi. I yearned their yearning and they yearned mine. I became the sesshin. When someone cried out, he cried out my pain. When another rushed to dokusan, he announced my eagerness. When the monitors wielded their sticks and breathed so heavily with their exertions, they breathed mu for me. The roshi's efforts were my efforts. An awful responsibility became mine. I could not let the sesshin down.

The struggle took on titanic proportions. "It is like a strong man taking a weak man by the shoulders and pushing him down," said the Buddha. Yes indeed, this is how it is. The energy necessary for this already had passed my own meager efforts. Mu, like the point of an arrow, was backed by all the will force I could muster, but then a new force came in. The force of the entire sesshin seemed to become focused in my hara. The shoulders, chest, arms, and stomach were all relaxed, but there was this mighty concentrating force at work.

The struggle was furious. Dry periods came, but my impatience was too much for them. It was just as though one were smashing through a wall. On the fifth day I rose at

2:00 a.m. and sat until 4:00 without moving, totally absorbed in mu. The pain in my legs was blinding and yet easily transformed into the questioning of mu. I rushed to dokusan but came back bewildered. Roshi had questioned me, had helped me, but when I came back a doubt about him arose. "He is going to pass me too easily. He is not deeply enlightened and doesn't want anyone else to be." The monitor struck me. It hurt. This whole Zen business is a hoax! Harada Roshi admitted that all he did was sell water by the river. He even admitted that he was a sham. There is nothing in it! This seemed like a clever pun and a stupid giggling rose up. But through the work period these nagging doubts continued and the desperation grew. If the roshi is no good, where do I go? I struggled with a sinking feeling of being all alone, utterly forsaken.

The teisho that morning cleared up my doubts completely. Roshi talked about the intellect, about how it is the servant, yet claims to be the master. I began to cry. He seemed to be talking to me alone. There were just he and I, and as he talked he seemed to be sawing, sawing, sawing away at my depths. I do not remember what he said, but it was very painful. The sawing went on and on and I was racked by sobs. It was surely this experience that made way for what was to come.

At dokusan on the last night, the roshi was again about to repeat to me his warning of the importance of the last day and the need for great effort. I interrupted him and said vigorously, "Yes, I know, I know, I will, I promise you I will, I'll do it!" And on leaving the dokusan room, I turned and flung out a final, "I will!" I had resolved to myself to sit up all night and pour myself simply into mu.

After the evening bell had rung and the closing cere-

mony performed, I sorted out a place in the zendo and started to do zazen, but found that my attention was scattered,
thoughts arose constantly, and I had a great deal of pressure
in my chest. I was sitting for at the most twenty-minute
rounds, and moving constantly. Again I fought with discouragement. I wandered restlessly around the zendo looking for a place to sit. I wandered downstairs, carrying my
cushion and sitting mat with me, but nowhere found the
place that would enable me to do the sitting that I wanted to
do. I returned to the zendo and felt utterly forlorn. It was
about midnight, and I thought it would be best to go to bed,
but remembered my vow to the roshi and myself and felt
very foolish. I tried unsuccessfully to crash through the
thoughts and the barrier they created. My sitting was
ragged, egoistic, and it seemed quite ineffective. But I could
not go to bed and although it seemed that the sitting I was
doing was pointless and having no effect, I nevertheless
struggled on. Finally at 2:30 a.m. I gave up and, full of
shame, went to bed.

Strangely, the next morning when the waking bell
rang, I slipped out of my sleeping bag with a feeling of cool
assurance. On getting to the mat I found that the sitting that
had been so earnestly sought the night before came with
great ease. Having at last got a grasp on mu, I decided not
to go to dokusan but instead to continue working at my
practice.

Once more the monitor came and told me to go to
dokusan. I went reluctantly and with a feeling of misgiving
about his having interrupted such good sitting. But, now
before the roshi, I found that answers could now be given
that had not been available before. The dokusan was a great
success and charged me with the resolve to work harder. At

the lunch break I was so tired that I sat on a chair downstairs and could not keep my head up. Nevertheless, I
worked hard until the bell rang for the afternoon zazen and
then, when dokusan came round, joined the line once more.
I had grasped my practice and was working furiously. On
going into the dokusan room, however, the roshi pointed
out that my answers were still too intellectual and were no
advance on what I had given in the morning. I was so tired
that I could hardly sit up on the dokusan mat.

Returning to the zendo I was totally discouraged and
felt I had to give up. I sat leaning forward and rested my
weight on my hands to prevent myself from falling over. I
had no energy and, it seemed, no will. However, the young
man on my right sat up straight and he was evidently working extremely hard. I thought, "He has not given up, so why
should I?" and by a total effort of will concentrated on
searching into mu in the hara, and my spine straightened of
itself and remained straight until the end of the sesshin.

Kensho

I was awakened at 2:00 a.m. on Sunday, the morning after
the rohatsu sesshin, by my wife closing the window. She
returned to bed and went to sleep, and my attention turned
inward to my inner state. With this turning inward I saw
that there was a closing, a tensing that arose from lack of
faith, and I resolved to have greater faith at future sesshins.
Then I decided to express this faith immediately by allowing
the closing to open. This opening was accompanied by a
feeling of falling and of fear.

At one time the roshi had urged on sesshin participants
by saying that they could not fall out of the universe, and
recalling this gave me the courage necessary to allow the

opening to continue. The feeling of falling went on and was accentuated by probing an ancient fear. A realization came that liberation was the freedom to suffer, not freedom from suffering. This insight speeded up the process, and the feeling of dying arose with a fear of death. (The word "process" is used for want of a better, although it gives the appearance of something happening. All that was happening was a "knowing.")

I said to myself, "I am dying, and if this is the case, then let me observe what happens." The feeling of fear and alarm increased until I noticed that my heart was beating, and the realization dawned that if my heart was beating, the process was not one of dying. I then found myself in a vast empty space, lit as it were by moonlight. I had a feeling of being completely at ease and of the feeling being perfectly natural, of just being at home. There was no exhilaration or exaltation, just a perfectly natural feeling. I realized with a complete but nevertheless unconcerned certainty that I could not possibly die.

I then turned to the possibility of going mad, and a new fear arose, accompanied by the feeling of being increasingly enmeshed. Again came the complete but unconcerned certainty that, although I could be in madness, I could not be mad. Once again the fear subsided.

Yet a new fear arose, and that was that if I could not die, I would suffer a form of cosmic insomnia. Along with this was the concern, is this all there is? And the answer came, "No, there is walking, talking, eating and sleeping." It was seen that Joshu's, "When I am hungry, I eat, and when I am tired, I sleep," had a new reality. (A normal man looks at his life of walking and sleeping and eating and asks, "Is this all there is?" He answers, "No, there is a higher life, the life of the void." From the life of the void I was asking, "Is this all there is?" and answering, "No, there is the life of existence.") The concern left me, and I remained alone in vast empty space.

There is no way in which the condition can be described other than being natural. It was not an "experience." There was nothing outside to "cause" the experience, nor was there an outside, just a wholeness and completeness. There was no feeling of needing to control anything, or of being in any way out of control. Perfect but natural liberation.

I then noticed the difference between knowing and thinking. The state was one of full knowing, like bright moonlight. There was nothing vague, unreal, or hazy about it. When thoughts arose it was as though a darkening took place; the knowing was more limited and tension was evident. I knew my wife was sleeping and I knew that if she were to awake she would disturb the process. This caused thoughts to arise. Eddies of thought clouded this knowing, and these eddies can only be likened to ripples on water on which the moon is shining.

There came the question, "What is happening?" A doubt arose. The *Prajnaparamita Sutra* came to mind. (How can one praise enough the patriarchs who have had us recite daily the *Prajnaparamita?*) The doubt gave rise to the need to validate the process, although I do not know why, and the *Prajnaparamita* became the means by which this validation could be done.

> *The Bodhisattva of compassion*
> *From the depths of prajna wisdom*
> *Saw the emptiness of all five skandhas*

And sundered the bonds that
Caused him suffering.

There was a looking round at the various ways of the senses, and with this came a sense of an inward crushing, of melting. (Later the process was described to my teacher as one of honeycombs being crushed and melted.) It seemed that the inner barriers were being crushed and melted. An awareness passed throughout my body, along my limbs, through my trunk, and lastly into my head. Wherever an obstruction rose it was melted in the process. This continued for some time.

Dharmas here are empty
All are the primal void.

This is the primal void!

None take birth or die.

This I saw as a clear and natural certainty. But at this point arose a doubt (a doubt that persists) and could be phrased by the questions, "Where does it all come from? Where is its source?"

Nor are they stained or pure
Nor do they wax or wane
So in emptiness no form
No feeling, thought or choice,
Nor is there consciousness;
No eye, ear, nose, tongue body, mind.
No color, sound, smell, taste, touch,

Or what the mind takes hold of,
Nor even act of sensing.

All of this I saw immediately and intuitively as being the case.

No ignorance, or end of it.

At this point I felt a knowing of the sin of ignorance, a weighing down at this point. I do not know what this weighing down was.

Nor all that comes of ignorance,
No withering, no death,
No end of them.

The part of no-death I had already seen, but the intuitive awareness confirmed once again: no-death.

Nor is there pain, or cause of pain
Or cease in pain, or noble path to
Lead from pain.
Not even wisdom to attain.

There is no wisdom, there is just "knowing"; not an empty knowing, but a "knowing" knowing.

Attainment too is emptiness
So know that the Bodhisattva
Holding to nothing whatever.

Alone in vast empty space, holding to nothing whatever.

But dwelling in prajna wisdom

This is the state of knowing.

Is freed of delusive hindrance
The waves, eddies, stilled.

Rid of the fear bred by it.

Each of the fears had been explored and dissolved.

And reaches clearest Nirvana.
All Buddhas of past and present,
Buddhas of future time,
Using this prajna wisdom,
Come to full and perfect vision.

The question of "come to full and perfect vision" raised a doubt. At this point the exploration of the sutra was ended with the clear knowing that what it described was precisely what was now occurring.

The process came slowly to an end through what seemed to be going to sleep, but turned out to be waking up. The clock registered 4:00 a.m. The whole process had lasted two hours.

My wife awakened about 4:30 a.m. I described to her in detail what had happened, much as it is written above. Already the reality of the world was supplanting the reality of the process, and doubts were arising about whether, in fact, I had been dreaming. I felt further need to validate what had occurred, and my wife and I turned to Hakuin's "Chant in Praise of Zazen." (Again the incomparable wisdom of the patriarchs.)

> *The gateway to freedom is zazen samadhi,*
> *Beyond exaltation, beyond all our praises,*
> *The pure Mahayana.*

Indeed, this had been a samadhi and indeed, because it was natural, it was beyond exaltation, it was pure mahayana.

> *Thus one true samadhi extinguishes evils,*
> *It purifies karma, dissolving obstructions.*

These same obstructions had been crushed and melted or dissolved like honeycomb in honey.

> *But if we turn inward and prove our true nature,*
> *That true self is no-self*
> *Our own self is no-self,*

This vast, empty, moonlit space is our true self; this void is our true self.

> *We go beyond ego and past clever words.*

There was no ego; there were no words.

> *Then the gateway to the oneness of cause-and-effect*
> *Is thrown open.*

There was doubt about the meaning of this.

Appendix Three

Not two and not three,
Straight ahead runs the Way.

There was doubt about this.

Now our form is no form

How can we describe the form of the void?

So in coming and going
We never leave Home.

This never leaving home is the naturalness of the process. Wherever we are, whatever we do, we are always natural to ourselves.

Now our thought is no-thought.

The distinction between knowing and thinking.

So our dancing and songs
Are the voice of the dharma.
How vast is the heaven of boundless samadhi.

Boundless indeed!

How bright and transparent
The moonlight of wisdom.

This describes the vast empty space, lit, as it were, by moonlight.

What is there outside us,
What is there we lack?

There was nothing outside, there was no outside, there was nothing lacking.

Nirvana is openly shown to our eyes.
This earth where we stand
Is the pure Lotus Land.

Is this all there is? No, there is also the talking, walking, sleeping, and eating. This earth where we stand.

And this very body of Buddha.

Ah!

My wife and I discussed at some length what we should do. We were due to meet our daughter in Toronto and had planned to leave with two other sesshin participants at about 5:00 that morning. After some hesitation we decided to wait to discuss the "process" with the roshi.

The hesitation arose because of increasing concern that what had happened was simply a dream, or makyo. I had no feeling of any greater insight or understanding of the koan Mu. I felt a sense of trepidation at displaying another experience to the roshi who has without doubt been bombarded by thousands of such experiences. I felt concern at causing the other two people to be delayed and of our waiting daughter. All, perhaps, for nothing. Furthermore, the roshi had conducted a severe rohatsu sesshin and deserved to be left alone. However, the question remained, what was this? and deep in my hara was an intuition. My wife also urged me to stay and see the roshi.

I found that the roshi would not be available until 7:00 or 8:00 that morning. I discussed questions of different kinds with a monk, drank tea, and became increasingly apprehensive as 7:00 o'clock came round. I had the constant nagging temptation to say, "Let's leave it; let's just go home."

My wife came to say that she had been packing the car and had seen that the roshi's lights were on. I went and knocked on his door. He called out, "Wait a moment. Who is there?" I gave my name. I felt sick. He opened the door and overcame my fumbled apologies with a compassionate welcome.

I apologized as I sat down, feeling foolish, and stuttered that I had some sort of experience and felt that it needed validation or rejection. He asked me what the experience had been, and after I had given a broad outline, he slowly probed and questioned until the story was fully told.

He was obviously interested, and rejected my suggestion that it might be makyo. He had listened intently and had questioned gently throughout, and some reassurance was growing in me that perhaps what had happened had some value more than a mere dream.

The roshi asked some questions about the koan Mu. I thought about the first question he asked and felt it didn't make sense. He tried again and asked another question. Again, the only answer that I could give was an intellectual one. He tried a third time, and I felt a restlessness stir in me. I stood up and walked away from him. The question suddenly went deep and an eruption, a volcano, roared up from the hara. I yelled at the top of my voice, "This is Mu! Mu!

Mu! Mu!" and danced and jigged and jumped up and down, pounded the floor with my fists, and flung myself on the ground, banging my head on the ground. I was yelling and laughing, "This is Mu! Lovely Mu! By God, this is Mu! This is Mu! This is Mu! Mu! Mu!" The paroxysm spent itself at last and my teacher, as compassionate as ever, said, "Yes indeed, you have seen into Mu."

Afterword

Eight or nine hours after leaving the roshi we arrived home, having picked up our daughter. That night was passed sleeplessly. Joyful peace, limitless, joyful peace. I was exhausted but could not sleep so great was my joy.

Throughout the rest of the week and beyond there has persisted the feeling of being unobstructed, of walking on my own feet, of seeing with my own eyes. Except for periods of profound gratitude toward the roshi, and the sesshin members, and my wife, it has all been natural, easy. The joy left, the peace left, leaving just a natural open feeling.

A veritable explosion had occurred, but debris remains. Old habits, mind states, reactions are still there. Irritation, anxiety, ambitions. But they have lost their grip. Old enemies rise up, crumble, and turn to dust, and that tyrant the old dead king is broken, he need be fed no longer.

It is as though something that was formerly tightly anchored is now adrift. Like a boil that has been lanced—still a bit painful but so easy; or like a sick man who has passed the crisis, he is getting well, he knows he is getting well, but he is still weak, and much work is yet necessary.

The practice has also changed. It has become deep and smooth, it is no longer something apart.

Appendix Three

Roshi's Response

Now that our solstice and New Year celebrations are over—
and the entertainment performances New Year's Eve would
do justice to any group of professional actors and musi-
cians—there is time to give you an unpremeditated response
to the events surrounding your kensho.

First, let me say how fortunate that you did not leave
the center at 4:00 a.m. the day after the sesshin, as you had
planned, but that you came to see me at 7:00. Your wife's
intuitions that you not leave without contacting me first
were so sound.

After a kensho, particularly one as stirring as yours,
frequently there is a letdown—what has been termed "the
post-kensho blues"–in which melancholia and gnawing
doubt often arise; their strength is in proportion to the
intensity of the initial joy and exultation. But if you persist
in your zazen, in fact intensify it, these negative mind states
usually clear up and give way to a clarity and certainty
unlike anything you have experienced before. Not to men-
tion a feeling of stability and rootedness. What is called for
at this crucial point is sustained sitting. Lingering doubts,
such as, "Is all this real? Will it persist?" do appear, but are
like a chicken whose head has been cut off but still continues to thrash about. This is not to say, of course, that your
understanding of mu is not capable of greater depth and
sureness. As you proceed in your post-kensho training, your
horizons with respect to mu will enlarge. You say, "There is
no feeling of any greater insight or understanding of the
koan Mu." But there was, you will recall, a positive demonstration of the spirit of the koan. And that is most important.

Dokusan at this point is vital. One is like a puppy that

has just opened its eyes on the world, it needs its mother's care and nourishment. So do try to come down for at least one dokusan before I leave for Costa Rica.

To you and your family in the New Year more peace and more joy.

Appendix Four

Indra's Net

This excerpt, part of the *Hwa Yen Sutra,* is from *The Buddhist Teaching of Totality* by Garma C. Chang, (University Park: The Pennsylvania State University, 1977) and is reproduced by permission of the publisher.

Fa Tsang, a proponent of the Hwa Yen, gave a demonstration of the teaching of the Hwa Yen to the empress of China. When he had made the necessary arrangements he went to the empress and said, "Your Majesty, I am now ready. Please come with me to a place where the demonstration will be given." He then led the empress into a room lined with mirrors. On the ceiling, on the floor, and on all four walls and even in the four corners of the room were fixed huge mirrors—all facing one another. Then Fa Tsang produced an image of Buddha and placed it in the center of the room with a burning torch beside it. "Oh, how fantastic! How marvelous!" cried the empress as she gazed at this awe-inspiring panorama of infinite inter reflections. Slowly and calmly Fa Tsang addressed her:

"Your Majesty, this is a demonstration of totality in the Dharmadhatu. In each and every mirror within this room you will find the reflections of all the other mirrors with the Buddha's image in them. And in each and every reflection of any mirror you will find all the reflections of all the other mirrors, together with the specific Buddha in each, without omission or misplacement. The principle of inter-penetration and containment is clearly demonstrated. Right here we see an example of one in all and all in one—the mystery of realm embracing realm ad infinitum is thus revealed. The principle of the simultaneous arising of different realms is so obvious here that no explanation is necessary. These infinite reflections of different realms now simultaneously arise without the slightest effort; they just naturally do so in a perfectly harmonious way.

"As for the principle of the nonobstruction of space, it can be demonstrated in this manner. . . . "(saying which, he took a crystal ball from his sleeve and placed it in the palm of his hand)." Your Majesty, now we see all the mirrors and their reflections within this small crystal ball. Here we have an example of the small containing the large as well as the large containing the small. This is the demonstration of the nonobstruction of sizes, or space.

"As for the nonobstruction of times, the past entering the future and the future entering the past cannot be shown in this demonstration, because this, after all, is a static one, lacking the dynamic quality of the temporal elements."

Notes on the Illustrations

page 54: Ink painting of Bodhidharma by Fugai in the Nishimura collection, Tokyo. The calligraphy, by Insan, reads:

From Eastern lands (China) came the very first
  (zen) teachings
Direct pointing from heart to heart.
Like the falcon's clear sight, the eagle's eye
Whose brilliance shattered the world.

pages 70, 109, 174, 228: Ink paintings by Elizabeth Namiesniowski.

page 137: Ink painting by Hakuin in the Hosokawa collection, Tokyo. The calligraphy reads:

A monkey grasps for the moon's reflection upon the water,
Not until death will he give up . . .
If he would just let go, he would
Plunge into the depths.
Clear shines the light in all directions.

page 218: Ink painting of the three laughing sages at Hu-ch'i (Kokei) by Bunsei, from the middle of the 15th century. It is reproduced from *Zen and Japanese Culture* by D. T. Suzuki (London: Routledge and Kegan and Paul, 1959).

Select Bibliography

Blyth, R. H. *Zen and Zen Classics Volume Four: The Mumonkan.* Tokyo: The Hokuseido Press, 1966.

Buber, Martin. *I and Thou.* Edinburgh: T. and T. Clark, 1937.

Chang, Garma C. *The Buddhist Teaching of Totality: The Philosophy of Hwa Yen Buddhism.* University Park: Pennsylvania State University Press, 1977.

Cleary, Thomas, ed. *The Original Face: An Anthology of Rinzai Zen.* New York: Grove Press, Inc., 1979.

Grant, Robert, M. *The Secret Sayings of Jesus: The Gnostic Gospel of Thomas.* New York: Doubleday & Co. Inc., 1960.

The Zen Teachingsof Huang Po: On the Transmission of Mind. Edited and translated by John Blofeld. Boston: Shambhala Publications, 1994.

Koestler, Arthur. *The Ghost in the Machine.* New York: Viking Penguin, 1990.

Low, Albert. *The Butterfly's Dream: In Search of the Spiritual Roots of Zen.* Boston: Charles E. Tuttle Co., Inc. 1993.

Low, Albert. *An Invitation to Practice Zen.* Rutland, Vermont: Charles E. Tuttle Co., Inc., 1989.

Low, Albert. *The Iron Cow of Zen.* Rutland, Vermont: Charles E. Tuttle Co., Inc., 1985

Low Albert. *Zen and Creative Management.* Rutland, Vermont: Charles E. Tuttle Co., Inc., 1976.
Maharaj, Nisargadatta. *I Am That: Talks with Sri Nisargadatta Maharaj.* Durham, North Carolina: Acorn Press, 1994.

Maxwell, Meg and Verena Tschudin. *Seeing the Invisible: Modern Religious and Other Transcendental Experiences.* London: Arkana Books, 1994.

Bibliography

Papels, Elaine. *The Gnostic Gospels*. New York: Vintage Books, 1981.

Price, A. F. and Wong Mou-Lam, trans. *The Diamond Sutra*. Berkeley: Shambhala Publications, 1974.

Saxena, Sushil Kumar. *Studies in the Metaphysics of Bradley*. London: Allen & Unwin, 1967.

Shannon, William, H. *Thomas Merton's Dark Path: The Inner Experience of Contemplation*. Harmonsworth: Penguin Books, 1982.

Shibayama, Zenkei. *Zen Comments on the Mumonkan*. New York: Harper & Row: New York, 1974

Shigematsu, Soiku, trans. and introduction. *A Zen Forest*. New York: Weatherhill, 1981

Stryk, Lucien and Takashi Ikemoto eds. *Japanese Zen: Poems, Prayers, Sermons, Anecdotes*. New York: Doubleday and Co., Inc., 1963.

Suzuki, D. T., ed. *A Manual of Zen Buddhism*. New York: Grove Atlantic, 1987

The Holy Teaching of Vimalakirti. Translated by Robert A. F. Thurman. University Park: The Pennsylvania State University Press, 1991.

Wu, John, trans. *The Golden Age of Zen*. Published by the National War College in cooperation with the Committee on the compilation of the Chinese Library.

Yun, Xu. *Empty Cloud: An Autobiography of the Chinese Zen Master*. Translated by Charles Luk, revised and edited by Richard Hunn. Rockport, Massachusetts: Element Books, Inc., 1990.

Zen Bow magazine is available by subscription from the Rochester Zen Center, 7 Arnold Park, Rochester, NY 14607.